W9-CKC-377

ओ३म्

Health Spirituality Culture Refinement Teaching

Brief Description of the Utility & Quality of Drugs (Ingredients) of the Patent & Classical Medicines Manufactured by '*Divya Pharmacy*' run by *DIVYA YOG MANDIR (TRUST)*

'*AYURVEDA*'

Philosophy of Eternal Health & Happiness

along with

Experienced Miraculous Remedies for Many Incurable Diseases Mentioned

By

Honourable Swami Ram Devji Maharaj

-: Editor :-

Vaidyaraj Acharya Balkrishna Ji Maharaj

DIVYA PHARMACY

Divya *Yog* Mandir (Trust)
Kripalu Bagh Ashram, Kankhal
Hardwar – 249408
Telephone : 01334-244107, 240008, 246737
Fax : 01334-244805

E-mail : divyayoga@rediffmail.com
Website : www.divyayoga.com

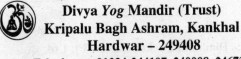

FIRST EDITION : 2005

'AYURVEDA' : Philosophy of Eternal Health & Happiness

ISBN 81-89235-24-9

Publisher : **DIVYA PRAKASHAN**
Divya *Yog* Mandir (Trust)
Kripalu Bagh Ashram, Kankhal
Hardwar – 249408

E-mail : divyayoga@rediffmail.com
Website : www.divyayoga.com
Telephone : 01334-244107, 240008, 246737
Fax : 01334-244805

Printer : **Sai Security Printers Limited**
152, DLF Industrial Area, Faridabad (Haryana) 121003
Tel. : 0129-2257743, 2270309, 2272277
Fax : 0129-2256239
E-mail: saipressindia@yahoo.com

Distributor : **Diamond Pocket Books (P). Ltd.**
X-30, Okhla Industrial Area, Phase-II,
New Delhi-110020
Phone: 011-41611861, Fax: 011-41611866
E-mail:sales@diamondpublication.com
Website:www.diamondpublication.com

ENGLISH 0123

Romanic Equivalents of *Devanāgarī*

Devanāgarī (Vowels) Initial	Medial	Roman Equivalents
अ	X	a
आ	ा	ā
इ	ि	i
ई	ी	ī
उ	ु	u
ऊ	ू	ū
ऋ	ृ	ṛ
ए	े	e
ऐ	ै	ai
ओ	ो	o
औ	ौ	au
अं	-	ṃ
:	-	ḥ

Devanāgarī Consonants

Devanāgarī Alphabets	Roman Equivalents	*Devanāgarī* Alphabets	Roman Equivalents
क	ka	ढ	ḍha
ख	kha	ण	ṇa
ग	ga	त	ta
घ	gha	थ	tha
ङ	ṅa	द	da
च	ca	ध	dha
छ	cha	न	na
ज	ja	प	pa
झ	jha	फ	pha
ञ	ña	ब	ba
ट	ṭa	भ	bha
ठ	ṭha	म	ma
ड	ḍa	-	-

Devanāgarī **Alphabets**	**Roman Equivalents**
य	ya
र	ra
ल	la
व	va
श	śa
ष	ṣa
स	sa
ह	ha
क्ष	kṣa
त्र	tra
ज्ञ	jña
श्र	śra

What is Ayurveda?

Ayurveda is not only a science of medicines, but also a theory of living a life with awareness. That is why Maharṣi Caraka Says :

'Trayopaṣṭambhā āhāra-nidrā-brahmacrarya iti !!

There are three factors supporting life viz. intake of food, sleep and observance of *brahmarcarya* (which includes control of senses and spiritual bliss conducive to the knowledge of Brahman).

Our body is a mirror of our food and thoughts. So, one should always lead his life being physically fit and happy by observing *brahmacrarya* (celibacy) which is our original nature, and is necessary for a health associated with consciousness.

Is the cause of your Disease One of the following :

1. Intake of meal without hunger, and eating in haste without chewing.
2. Eating frequently and more than one's own requirement.
3. Intake of food which is not suitable to our constitution (*prakṛti*).
4. Excessive intake of spicy things, tea, coffee, sugar, bread, pawroṭī and synthetic food under the influence of our impulses.
5. Intake of food under excitement, grief, anger, anxiety, disgust and tension.
6. Sleeping late at night and rising late in the morning.
7. Lack of physical exercise and leading a unrestrained life.
8. Intake of prohibited things like meat, alcohol, tobacco, etc.

Awareness about the preservation as well as promotion of positive health by default leads to the prevention of much dreaded diseases.

- Vaidyaraj Balkrishan Ji Maharaj

Dawn of New Revolution in the Ayurvedic Tradition of Ancient Seers

The modern science of medicine (Allopathic system) has failed to cure a number of diseases of the present times. In spite of scientific researches, treatment of many diseases has failed to bear any fruit and such diseases are, therefore, being considered as incurable. The methods of treatment developed so far, only take care of the manifested symptoms like pain etc. They do not root out the original disease. After subsidence, such symptoms reappear. Some diseases have been declared as incurable viz. diabetes, rheumatism, osteo-arthritis, gout (rheumatism and arthritis), migraine, cervical spondylitis, respiratory disorders, asthma, cancer, etc. Nervous disorders, heart diseases and diseases of brain like epilepsy etc. are also the diseases of same category.

Vaidyaraj Acharya
Shri Bal Krishan Maharaj

In respect of these diseases which are considered incurable in the modern medical system, the ancient sages had prescribed successful treatment. In line with the treatment of those sages, deep study of the classics, and with the grace of God, works related to upliftment, development and research in the field of Ayurveda, have been undertaken with full dedication by the *Brahmakalpa Cikitsālaya* (Hospital) controlled by '**Divya Yog Mandir Trust**'. The Trust is situated within the premises of Kripalu Bagh Ashram on the branch of Ganga Canal in Kankhal area of Hardwar. Along with the hospital, there is a factory (***Divya Pharmacy***) for manufacturing medicines in pure form. There is also a vast botanical garden in which herbal plants, useful in the treatments of diseases, are planted. Many scarce medicinal plants have been grown with great care after research. In the near future, the hospital, botanical garden and the factory are being accorded grand and extensive look. Among the major service projects run by the Ashram, the Yog Service Project is being organized earnestly under the able guidance of the ascetic Yogiraj Swami Ram Devji Maharaj whereas the great Ayurvedic treatment and research work is being carried on under the supervision of Acharya Shri Balkrishan Ji Maharaj. Here, along with the Ayurvedic medicines, practical training in *Āsanas, Prāṇāyāmas*, other Yogic exercises and Acupressure is also being imparted to the patients as per need. By his selfless services from day to night, most venerable adorable Acharya Shri Balkrishanji Maharaj is providing immense relief to the millions of patients suffering from innumerable physical and mental ailments, and is also guiding them in practising the art of enjoying healthy, disease free and blissful life. In fact, he is a sparkling star on the worldly horizon of the Ayurvedic Medical World. By his penance, practice and constant research, he, by means of pious herbs of the Himalayas, has for the first time in the world, discovered permanent cure for the complicated diseases like high blood pressure. By relieving the pain of the grief-stricken man by means of medical treatment, he is proving himself true to the dictum of the ancient sages –

"Kāmaye duḥkha-taptānām prāṇinām arti-nāśanam."

During the full year, about one to one and a half lakh patients are being benefitted by coming to the Ashram, whereas more than the above mentioned number of people are being cured of various ailments by using the medicines manufactured in the Ashram after receiving the same through postage,. etc.

Whereas respectful Acharyaji is always fully engaged by devoting his entire time in the Ayurvedic treatment of both curable and incurable diseases, thereby curing lakhs of people, his compassionate heart, polite behaviour, abundant love and sympathetic attitude has been a source of positive thinking and divine inspiration for the innumerable people. This has also led them forward to their spiritual upliftment in life. Acharya ji has associated with himself a strong team of about two dozens able physicians so as to cope with the medical humanitarian work on a large scale, which is proving beneficial not only to the whole of India but also to the people of many other countries, which includes learned, celebrated people and the common man.

Even senior physicians of the renouned medical institutions of India came here for the sake of treatment. Moreover, they also refer to **'Divya Yog Mandir'**, such cases of patients who suffer from incurable diseases, whose effective treatment is not available anywhere else in the world.

The following Vedic reference in respect of a physician applies fully to him:

"Ayaṃ me hasto Bhagavān, ayaṃ me hasto Bagavattaraḥ."

Many patients suffering from incurable diseases after getting cured, express their gratitude and regard to him. We offer our hundreds of salutations to this great saint wholly dedicated to the welfare of all humanity.

Dr. B.D. Sharma
(Former Head of the National Genetic Bureo, Phagali, Simla)
Shri Upendra Bhai Thakkar (Ahmedabad)
& all the devotees benefited by
Shri Jeevraj Bhai Patel (Surat)
Acharya ji's benefications

It is futile to derive happiness, satisfaction and tranquility while enjoying materialistic things, as is the thought to douse the fire by pouring ghee over it.

- Honourable Swami Ram Devji Maharaj

INTRODUCTION

DIVYA YOG MANDIR (TRUST), KANKHAL

The headquarter of the **Divya Yog Mandir Trust** is situated at Kankhal in the Kripalu Bag Ashram. The Kripalu Bag Ashram was founded in A.D. 1932 by Sh. Swami Kripalu Ji Maharaj, who originally belonged to Mewar (Rajasthan) which is the land of the brave. Before saṃnyāsa, his name was Yati Kishor Chand. In the struggle of Independence he played an active and successful role of a revolutionary. In Hardwar, he gave a shelter to thousands of revolutionaries. The name of local freedom fighter Veniprasad 'Jijñāsu' was among his chief supporters. Yati Kishor Chand founded the first Public library in Hardwar. He collected three thousand five hundred books with a lot of hardwork, and kept them in this library, situated at upper road. In order to activate the National Development Plan, he opened many schools in this area. He had a cordial and strong relationship with the founder of Gurukul Kangri University Swami Shraddhanand Ji. Later, he came in contact with Bal Gangadhar Tilak, Madan Mohan Malaviya, Moti Lal Nehru, Mahatma Gandhi, Chitaranjan Das, Ganesh Shanker Vidyarthi, V.J. Patel & Hakeem Ajmal Khan.

Yati Kishor Chand joined the *Bang Viplav Dal*. He took up the dangerous responsibility of increasing the popularity of two newspapers viz., ***'Yugāntara'*** and ***'Lokāntara'*** published by his group. These two newspapers which were published in the Bengali and English languages became great irritants to the Britishers. These newspapers which used to spit fire and create revolutionary thoughts among the masses, frightened the British Government greatly. Nobody knew from where these papers were published and distributed. Yati Kishor Chand used to pack these newspapers in packets and post them throughout India either from Hardwar's Chandi Pahar, or Nildhara Talhati or from his own library situated in Palival Dharmashala. In those days, Bang Viplav Dal performed the ***'Lord Harding Bomb Kand'*** from Delhi whose leader was Ras Bihari Bose. Yati Kishor Chand was given the responsibility of providing shelter to Ras Bihari Bose in Hardwar. The British Govt. had put a prize of Rs. Three lakhs on Ras Bihari Bose. Yati Kishor Chand hid him in his own Ashram situated in the middle of a jungle. Then Harish Babu, a friend of Yati Chand along with three other companions came to Hardwar and told him that the British suspected that Ras Bihari Bose was hiding in Hardwar or Dehradun and that there could be a raid at any time. Then

Yati Chand sent them to Banaras through Dehradun Express dressed as Patiyali passengers at night. The following morning, Yati Chand's Cottage was surrounded by the police. The police searched for Ras Bihari Bose in every nook & corner of that cottage, but the lion had escaped from the trap to Banaras and from there to Japan safely.

After then Yati took sanyas and later was called Kripalu Dev Maharaj. To rise national sentiments amongst the masses of British India, he published a monthly magazine – ***'Viśvajñāna'***. Yati had always lived a life of a freedom fighter and revolutionary. Now his interest rose in Yog and spirituality, and he became a Siddha Yogi. In 1968 A.D., he bid goodbye to this world.

The responsibility of the land of revolutions, Yog, meditation and spirituality fell into the hands of the pupils of Yati. Shri Swami Shankar Dev Ji is a part of this tradition whose worthiest student is Swami Ram Dev Ji who lit this Ashram with the divine light of Yog, Ayurveda and Vedic culture and made it famous in India and abroad quarter of the world. He founded ***'Divya Yog Mandir (Trust)'*** in 1995, and finalized the various plans and schemes of services through his closest associates and intimates like Ācārya Bāla Kṛṣṇa Jī, Swāmī Muktānanda Jī. His these achievements deeply influenced the hearts of the Indians. It is due to these efforts, the divine *Triveṇī* of these Vedas, Yog and Ayurveda has started flowing throughout India. Due to the influence of these saintly souls, thousands of people have been and being benefitted with physical health, mental peace, spiritual upliftment and intellectual consciousness. Each and every moment of the life of Swami Ram Dev Ji is being spent in the performance of these virtuous divine activities. He is equally progressive in every field of religion, Yog, spirituality, social services, education and welfare of all beings. Still this sage is working without any ego or pride thinking that he is only an instrument and whatever is being done or is to be performed is only due to the kindness and will of God.

- ***Promotion of Service-schemes : Through Divya Yog Mandir (Trust)***

During this short period of less than a decade, ***Divya yog Mandir (Trust)*** the milestones of achievements built through various service schemes of ***'Divya Yog Mandir (Trust)'*** have made the people to feel that all these achievements are not less than any divine miracle. The multifarious schemes (plans) being established in the form of ***'Patañjali Yogapīṭha'*** are making people to think that Swami Ram Dev Ji has definitely attained some divine achievement. Actually, this is the miraculous outcome of the devotion to God, the idea of sacrifice, a wish to serve the people and goodwill of universal welfare with which Swami

Ram Dev ji is always abound inspired and activated. The brief description of the different service plans of ***Divya Yog Mandir (Trust)*** is given below:

- ***Organising the Camps of Yoga-sādhanā & Yogic Treatments***

The camps of *Yoga-sādhanā* and Yogic treatment organized in the whole country by Swami Ram Dev Ji has eradicated this misgiving that *yoga* is something which only concerns with physical exercises. By applying this *yoga-sādhanā* as the base of physical health, cure of diseases, mental peace, self development, intellectual consciousness and spiritual upliftment, Swami Ram Dev Ji has given a special and supernatural significant meaning and definition to the word '*Yoga*'. This wonderful experience is directly being felt by the regular *sādhakas* of yogic practices. *Aṣṭāṅga-yog* (*yoga* consisting of eight parts viz. *Yama, Niyama, Āsana, Prāṇāyāma, Pratyāhāra, Dhāraṇā, Dhyāna & Samādhi*) prescribed by Maharṣi Patañjali is being taught and practised in these camps. Now arrangements are being made to train the people in practical studies and training of *Haṭha-yoga* along with *yoga-sūtras* of Pantañjali's *yoga-darśana* as per utility based on philosophy, *Upaniṣads, Caraka-saṃhitā, Suśruta-saṃhitā*, etc. It is also being arranged to give practical training of *Dhyāna-yoga* and *Japa-yoga* along with *Ṣaṭ-karma* (six purificatory acts belonging to *yoga* viz. *neti, dhauti, basti, trāṭaka, nauli & kapāla-bhāti*).

- ***Brahma-Kalpa Cikitsālaya***

Along with the teaching of Yogic *Ṣaṭ-karma* (as mentioned above), newly occurred and chronic diseases are being treated through this *Brahma-kalpa Cikitsālaya* (Hospital) by applying *pañca-karma* therapy (five eliminating therapies viz., massage, fomentation, emesis, purgation and *śiro-basti* elimination of *doṣas* from the head) prescribed in ayurveda, administering ayurvedic medicines containing herbs, *rasas* (metallic medicines) and *rasāyanas* (rejuvenators), proper diet and regimens, following wholesomeness and unwholesomeness, observing balanced celibacy and by correcting *ṛtu-caryā* (conduct during different reasons) as well as *dina-caryā* (regimen during day time).

In this *Brahmakalpa Cikitsālaya*, chronic and palliable diseases, like high blood pressure, diabetes mellitus, heart-diseases, asthma, obesity, acidity, allergy, ulcer, cervical spondylitis, sciatica, arthritis, cancer (in first and second stages) are being cured without operation.

Efforts are being made to convert this hospital into a big medical centre where the patients will be accommodated for the treatment in a particular way.

Swami ji insists that we should try to teach the people how to be free from the diseases and whenever they fall sick, should try to treat themselves with the help of yogic system. If medicine is needed, people should preferably try to use Ayurvedic system because it is related to our soil, culture and nature, and is harmless. But for this, pure medicines of good quality are essential. So, for making available medicines of good quality at cheap rates, ***Divya Yog Mandir Trust*** has established ***Divya Pharmacy*** in the Ashram premises, where absolutely pure medicines of good quality are prepared in accordance with the procedure prescribed in the *śāstras*, viz. patent medicines are prepared in various forms, viz., *bhasmas* (calcined powders, *piṣṭīs*, medicines with gold, metallic medicines, *rasāyanas* (rejuvenators), *vaṭīs* (tablets & pills), *guggulu* (medicines containing *guggulu* or *Commiphora mukul* in abundance, *cūrṇa* (powders of herbs, etc.), linctus, *sat* (extracts), *kvātha* (decoction), *ghṛta* and *taila* (medicated ghee & oils prepared by boiling the paste, juice, etc. of different drugs), *lauha* (medicines containing iron in procuse quantity), *maṇḍūra* (medicines containing iron-rust in profuse quantity), *maṇḍūra* (medicines containing iron-rust in profuse quantity), *parpaṭī* (scale preparations), etc. We are trying our best that medicines should be pure and should be prepared according to the proper method so that they may contain all qualities as mentioned in the classics. Our effort is that common man can get these medicines at a minimum cost. However, output (of these medicines) is limited, that is why sometime people do not get these medicines, and are disappointed.

Therefore, actions are being taken for the expansion of this *Divya Pharmacy* as soon as possible, so that we may fulfil the needs and expectations of all the people.

- ***Laboratory***

Divya Yog Mandir (Trust) has its own laboratory. In spite of manufacturing and research of traditional medicines, its work has been expanded in various aspects, as follows :

- Search of new herbs
- Search of those herbs which are not available for years (a long period)
- To test the qualities of herbs & other ingredients bought for pharmacy
- To decide and determine the process by which medicines might be prepared according to the proper method as prescribed in classics
- To have the full and accurate knowledge about researches being ‹one in the fields of treatment and pharmacology as well as developing modern technology
- To buy the published and written literature on Ayurveda
- To write and publish the new literature;

◆ To protect and develop the herbal plants; and

◆ To commercialize the product.

We have created a hubbub by manufacturing many new self-experienced medicines in our laboratory. It has been found that because of unfavourable nature, four herbal plants of *Aṣṭa-varga* (a group of herbs containing eight plants, viz. *jīvaka, ṛṣabhaka, medā, mahā-medā, kākolī, kṣīra-kākolī, ṛddhi* & *vṛddhi*) had lost their existence and identity, because of their non-availability since hundreds of years. But the scholars of laboratory have found these four lost herbs in the very cold Himalayan ranges with a lot of hard work, deep interest and great devotion. There is a detailed description of these sought herbs in a book on *Aṣṭa-varga*, published by Trust in both languages, Hindi and English.

● ***Divya Herbal Garden***

From the very beginning, valuable efforts have been made in the Ashram for giving knowledge and for the protection and development of useful as well as invigorating herbs which are easy as well as difficult to find in India and abroad including Himalayan ranges. But because of the lack of place, it was not possible to convert this work into expanded and desired form. Now in *Patañjali Yogpīṭha*, we have sufficient land for this work. So, there is a planning to grow and protect these herbs on a larger scale. In near future, we will get fresh leaves, juice, root and fruits of these herbal plants as per need for the treatment. Plants in pots, and seeds will be provided for sale.

● ***Establishment of Divya Cowshed***

There was already a preplanning to serve, protect and develop the race of Indian Cows for getting their milk, ghee, urine, drug, etc. which are very useful in the preparation of ayurvedic medicines. But now this plan is being expanded according to which thousands of cows will be murtured in *Patañjali Yogapīṭha*. Cow-dung obtained from them will be used as compost and organic fertilizers so that we may get pure grains, fruits, vegetables and milk free from chemicals. There is a plan of preparing bio-gas with cow-dung which will fulfil the other needs of Ashram. These native cows will also be cross bred to improve their quality/breed so that those may be given honour and value.

● ***Performance of Yajña (Agnihotra)***

Actually *agnihotra* is a science in itself. It has been playing a special role in Indian tradition for different purposes viz., for the purification and maintenance of balance in environment, making seasons favourable, developing and protecting crops, controlling the loss and excess of rains, treatment of some diseases, and for the completion of religious and spiritual rituals. This tradition of *yajña* started by *ṛṣis* is meant ideal. So, daily *yajña* (*agnihotra*) is performed in the Ashram. For this purpose, there is a provision to built a big *yajña-śālā* (place for performing *yajña*) in *Patañjali yogapīṭha*. There is a planning for scientific research, test and studies on these beneficial points as mentioned above.

- ***Vedic Gurukula***

This Trust is running a *Vidyātīrtha Gurukula* which is situated in Kishangadh Ghaseda, 8 km. far away from Revari City of Haryana free of cost, and high modern education is being given in this *gurukula* along with the teachings of vedic culture, good *saṃskāras* (refinements) and high ideals so that, we may impart education along with good *saṃskāras* to children (students) coming from high class families as well as the families from villages, folk and poor ones. Still there is a need to construct a building so that more children may be accommodated and receive education.

- ***Sādhanā Aśrama in Gaṅgotrī***

Divya Yog Mandir (Trust) has constructed a Ashram in *Gaṅgotrī* for curious *sādhakas*, and for the research as well as the protection of scarce herbs found in Himalayan region. This Ashram needs to be in a wide and extensive form.

- ***Establishment of Patañjali*** **Yog-pīṭha**

Patañjali Yog-pīṭha is a multifarious planning of Mother Institute-***Divya Yog Mandir (Trust)***, Kankhal, which will take an embodiment in an area more than one thousand *bīghā*. This *yogpīṭha* will play an important role in the propagation, teaching, training and research of *Vedas*, *Yoga* and *Ayurveda*. It will provide residential facilities for two thousands (approx.) *sādhakas* and *sādhikās*. This extensive institute will contain two thousands and five hundred (approx.) rooms, buildings and halls which will be associated with pharmacy, hospital, cow-shed, herbal garden, divisions for publishing monthly magazine-'*Yoga-sandeśa*' and other literature as well as sale and research centers, library, printing press, kitchen, Yog-centre and *yajña-śālā* (place for performing *yajña*) accommodated with modern facilities. In this premises, people will get pure and *sāttvika* food which will be absolutely free from L.P.G. gas, chemical fertilizers and insecticides. This premises will develop as a self-dependant and self-reliant institution like *Śānti Niketana* of world famous poet Dr. Ravindra Nath Tagore. This will provide the means of health, yog-practice, mental peace and spiritual elevation for crores of people, and will be a world famous institution in the form of reverential land of austerity.

Swami Ram Dev Ji has auspicious resolution to fulfil this extensive multifarious planning in the budget of Rs. Hundred crores with the financial help of his crores of Indian *Sādhakas* and *Sādhikās* of Yog, which is being accomplished gradually by the great inspiration and grace of God-Our Almighty Father.

For the membership of this *Yoga-pīṭha*, the Trust has fixed the amount which is categorized as follows:

1.	Founder Member	-	5,00,000/-
2.	Patron member	-	2,51,000/-
3.	Life member	-	1,00,000/-
4.	Special (VIP, Chief) member	-	51,000/-
5.	Revered member	-	21,000/-
6.	Ordinary member	-	11,000/-

● ***Publication of Yoga-Sandesa (Monthly Hindi Magazine)***

Keeping in view the demand of thousands of *sādhakas* and *sādhikās* concerned with Divya Yog Mandir (Trust). *Yoga-sandeśa* a monthly magazine has been started to publish since Sept. 2003 under the supervision of experienced editors. Thousands of people are its monthly members which proves its popularity. In the present, 25,000 of its copies are circulated, which will increase upto the number of one lakh in near future. In this magazine, articles and poems related to Vedas, Yog, Ayurveda, Indian culture and refinement are published, and the outlines of the activities and future plannings of the Trust as well as the experiences of the readers are given. The rapid propagation of this Hindi Magazine during this short period is only a result of an extraordinary efficiency of Swami Ram Dev Ji.

WARNING - The remedies mentioned in this book are based on the qualitative medicines manufactured in ***Divya Pharmacy*** after the experiences of many gained in our Dispensary. Be careful that patients suffering from complicated diseases should not treat themselves merely on the basis of this book. They should take treatment after consulting with an authentic physician.

CONTENTS

Sr. No	Subject	Page No.

CHAPTER - I
SELF-EXPERIENCED (PATENT) MEDICINES

CHAPTER - IV
MIRACULOUS HOME REMEDIES FOR DIFFERENT DISEASES PRESCRIBED BY SWAMI RAM DEV JI IN YOG – CAMPS

CHAPTER - V
WHOLESOME & UNWHOLESOME DIET & REGIMENS FOR DIFFERENT DISEASES

Miscellaneous – Mode of Administration of Different Forms of Medicines in General (Tablets & Powders, *Bhasma*, *Āsava* & *Ariṣṭa*, *Kvātha* or Decoction), Acupressure, Massage, Steam-bath with Decoction (*Kvātha-snāna*), *Yogāsanas* & *Prāṇāyāma*

APPENDICES

- Appendix – I

  Names of Medicines Described in the Text.

- Appendix – II

  Botanical / English Equivalents of the Names of Drugs & Ingredients Used in The Text Given in Skt. / Hindi / Folk Languages.

- Appendix – III

  Names of Diseases for Which Medicines are Prescribed

- Rate-List of Patent Medicines

- Comparative Price of Different Forms of Medicines (Through Graphic Charts)

- Literature & Audio-Video Cassetts, etc. Published by *DIVYA* YOG MANDIR (TRUST)

- Rules to Place the Orders of Medicines, etc. from the Ashram

CHAPTER - I
SELF – EXPERIENCED (PATENT) MEDICINES

(1) *DIVYA* ARŚA KALPA VAṬĪ

Main Ingredients : *Rasāñjana* or pure *rasaunt*, *harītakī* or *jangh harad*, seeds of sweet variety of *nimba* (*bakayan*), bark of soap-nut, traditional *karpūra* (camphor), *kaharava* (umber), *khūna-kharābā* (dragon's blood), *kākamācī* (*makoy*), *ghṛta-kumārī, nāga-dauna.*

Therapeutic Uses :

(1) Cures both types of piles viz., bleeding piles, & dry piles, relieves related complications like pain, burning sensation and colic pain.

(2) Protects fistula-in-ano if taken for some days regularly.

Mode of Administration : To be taken with butter-milk or water on empty stomach in the morning and in the evening before dinner.

Dosage : 1-2 tabs. twice a day, depending upon the seriousness of the diseases.

(2) *DIVYA* AŚMARĪ-HARA KVĀTHA

Main Ingredients : *Pāṣāṇa-bheda*, *go-kṣura*, root of *punarnavā*, *kulatthī*, bark of *varuṇa*.

Therapeutic Uses :

(1) Diuretic, cold & curative of oedema (anti-oedemous), especially strengthens excretory system.

(2) Dissolves the stones of kidney and urinary bladder and takes them out through urine; also useful for persons suffering from frequent formation of stones, as it stops the formation of stone. Cures the internal infections of kidney as well as other complications related there to. Also very useful in the stones of gall-bladder.

Mode of Administration : Take two teaspoonfuls (10 gms. approx.) of this dry decoction, boil with 500 ml. (1/2 glass) of water till it remains one-fourth, strain it out, and then take along with '*Aśmarī-hara Rasa*' (No.3).

Dosage : To be taken twice on empty stomach – in the morning and in the evening at about 6-7 0' clock before dinner.

(3) *DIVYA* AŚMARĪHARA RASA

Main Ingredients : *Yava-kṣāra, mūlī-kṣāra, śveta-parpaṭī, hajarala yahūda*, etc.

Therapeutic Uses :

(1) It is in powder form & is diuretic; dissolves deposited calculi & takes it out from the body; relieves complications as well as pains caused by it; removes oedema & pain of kidney; stops the tendency of stone formation. If used regularly for sometime, patient gets relieved for ever & no chance remains for stone-formation.

(2) Cures the burning sensation in the urine, & takes out deposited toxins from the body.

Mode of Administration : To be taken on empty stomach in the morning and in the evening at about 6-7 0' clock, either followed by '*Aśmarī-hara Kvātha*' or fresh water.

Dosage : 1-2 gm., twice a day.

(4) *DIVYA* UDARĀMṚTA VAṬĪ

Main Ingredients : *Punarnavā, bhūmyāmalakī* (*bhumi amala*), *kāka-mācī* (makoy), *citraka*, *āmalakī* (*amala*), *bibhītaka* (*baheda*), *trivṛt* (*nishoth*), *kuṭakī*, seed of *āmra* (mango), *bilva*, *ajamodā* (*ajavayan*), *ativiṣā* (*atis*) of bitter var., *ghṛta-kumārī* (Aloe), *muktā-śukti bhasma*, *kāsīsa bhasma*, *lauha bhasma*, *śaṅkha bhasma*, *maṇḍūra bhasma*, etc.

Therapeutic Uses :

1. Cures all types of abdominal diseases including abdominal pain, suppression of the power of digestion, indigestion, liver-diseases (e.g. jaundice), anaemia, chronic fever, diarrhoea and constipation.

Mode of Administration : To be taken in the morning after breakfast (or lunch) and dinner with luke warm water or milk.

Dosage : 1-2 tabs. twice a day.

(5) *DIVYA* UDARA-KALPA CŪRṆA

Main Ingredients : *Madhu-yaṣṭī (mulethi), miśreyā (saunf), svarṇa-patrī (sanay), revana-cīnī, śata-patrī* (rose-flower), *harītakī (jangh harad), miśrī* (sugar-candy) etc.

Therapeutic Uses :

(1) It is *pitta*-alleviating, mild purgative & non-evacing medicine.

(2) Clears bowls and removes constipation, doesn't cause any type of burning or other complication in intestines.

(3) Stimulates digestion, & digests *āma* (undigested material caused by impaired digestion & metabolism).

Mode of Administration : To be taken at bed time with warm water/ milk.

Dosage : 2-4 gms. (½-1 teaspoonful) etc.

Note : As it contains sugar-candy, as is prohibited for the patients suffering from diabetes. Being mild purgative, it is also safe for children.

(6) *DIVYA* KĀYĀ-KALPA VAṬĪ

Main Ingredients : Extracts of *bākucī* or *bavachi, cakra-marda (panavad), nimba, triphalā* (a collective name for *harītakī, bibhītakī & āmalakī*), *khadira, mañjiṣṭhā, kaṭukī, amṛtā, kirāta-tikta (chirayata), candana, deva-dāru, haridrā (haldi), dāru-haridrā, uṣbā, droṇa-puṣpī, laghu-kaṇṭakārī, kṛṣṇa-jīraka (kālājīrī)*, root of *indrāyaṇa*, seed of *karañja*, etc.

Therapeutic Uses :

(1) Purifies blood, so cures all types of skin-diseases successfully.

(2) Removes acne, pimples, dark spot on checks & spots on the face.

(3) Cures all types of chronic & complicated ring-worms (*dadru*), itches, pruritus & eczema instantaneously. It is complete cure for leucoderma & psoriasis as well.

Mode of Administration : To be taken twice on empty stomach in the early morning & one hour before dinner along with fresh water.

Precaution : Don't take milk or milk-preparations one hour before & after the intake of this medicine.

(7) *DIVYA* KĀYĀ-KALPA TAILA

Main Ingredients : Seeds of *bākucī* or *bavachi*, seeds of *cakra-marda* or *panavad*, *dāru-haridrā*, *haridrā*, seeds of *karañja*, bark of *nimba*, *harītakī* or *harad*, *āmalaka* or *amala*, *mañjiṣṭhā*, *amṛtā* (*giloy*), *kirāta-tikta* or *chirayata*, *kuṭakī*, *śveta-candana*, *deva-dāru*, *kṛṣṇa-jīraka* (*kali-jiri*), *droṇa-puṣpī*, *kaṇṭakārī*, *uṣbā*, *ariṣṭaka* (soap-nut), cow's urine, *tila-taila* (sesame oil).

Therapeutic Uses :

(1) Curses quickly all types of skin-diseases, like ring-worm (*dadru*), itching, eczema, leucoderma, proriasis, urticaria, freckles, skin allergy & sun-burning.

(2) Gives quick relief in cracks of hands & feet, burns, cuts & wounds. This oil is extremely useful & beneficial, so it should always be kept in each & every home.

Mode of Administration : To be applied twice or thrice a day on affected parts.

(8) *DIVYA* KĀYĀ-KALPA KVĀTHA

Main Ingredients : Seeds of *bākucī* (*bavachi*), *cakra-marda* (*panavad*), *haridrā* (turmeric), *dāru-haridrā*, bark of *khadira*, seeds of *karañja*, bark of *nimba*, *mañjiṣṭhā*, *amṛtā* (*giloy*), *kirāta-tiktaka* (*chirayata*), *kuṭakī*, *candana*, *deva-dāru*, *uṣbā*, *droṇa-puṣpī*, etc.

Therapeutic Uses :

(1) Cures all types of skin-diseases, eczema, *kuṣṭha* (obstinate skin diseases including leprosy), *ślīpada* (filariasis).

(2) Cleans bowels & helps in reducing obesity.

(3) Useful in skin-diseases along with '*Kāyā-kalpa Vaṭī*', and in obesity along with '*Medo-hara Vaṭī*'.

Mode of Administration : Boil 5-10 Gms. (1-2 teaspoons) of this dry decoction with 400 ml. of water till 100 ml. remains, and strain it out. Take on empty stomach in the morning and one hour before dinner. It is bitter in taste, so can be sweetened by adding honey, sugar or jaggery. Diabetic patient should not add any sweetner. If one cann't take it in more quantity, it can be concentrated by boiling more to have less quantity.

Dosage : 100ml., twice a day.

Note: It will be more effective if soaked in water for 8-10 hours before boiling.

(9) *DIVYA* KEŚA TAILA

Main Ingredients : *Bhṛṅga-rāja, brāhmī, āmalakī* (*amala*), *śveta candana, dāru-haridrā, kamala* (lotus), *ananta-mūla, ketakī, jaṭā-māṃsī, nīlinī* (indigo), *ratan-jot, guñjā*-white var. (*rattī*-white var), *priyaṅgu, lodhra, nāga-keśara, musta* (*nagar-motha*), *balā*, sesame oil, etc.

Therapeutic Usage :

(1) It is like a nectar for hair; cures untimely hair-fall, dandruff, alopecia, premature graying of hair, etc. By applying this oil, hair becomes healthy & luxurious.

(2) As it is prepared with many celestial herbs, it also strengthens eyes & brain, as well as cools the brain.

(3) Also useful in headache & different types of head-diseases.

Mode of Administration : Apply it in the hair-roots, massage well. To have more effects, it should not be washed away.

(10) *DIVYA* GAISA-HARA CŪRṆA

Main Ingredients : *Ajamodā* (*ajavayan*), *marica* (black pepper), extract of lemon, *jīraka* (cummin seed), black salt, *jaṅgha harītakī, hiṅgu* (pure), etc.

Therapeutic Uses :

(1) Digests food, so there is no occurrence of gas, acidity, etc. caused by indigestion.

(2) Instantaneously cures feeling of heaviness of abdomen, flatulence, colic pain and anorexia after food.

(3) This *cūrṇa* keeps away the gas of abdomen.

Mode of Administration : To be taken after food with luke-warm water; also can be taken at any time on the occurrence of complaints, like abdominal pain, flatulence, uneasiness, etc.

Dosage : ½ teaspoon, two times a day or as required.

(11) *DIVYA* CŪRṆA

Main Indredients : Rose flower, dry ginger, rock-salt, leaves of *svarṇa-patrī* (*sanay*), *jaṅgha harītakī* (*harad*), *kṛṣṇa-bījā* (*kālā-dānā*), *miśreyā* (*saunf*).

Therapeutic Uses :

(1) Cures constipation & takes out the faeces adhered in the intestines; activates intestines, so the internal layer of intestines does not allow the faeces to adhere there again.

(2) Totally clears the stomach; removes disappointment & makes the body active.

(3) Helps in curing abdominal pain, flatulence, heaviness & nausea.

Mode of Administration : To be taken at bed time with warm water.

Dosage : One teaspoonful (5 gms.).

(12) *DIVYA* PEYA (HERBAL TEA)

Main Ingredients : *Elā* (cardamom), *teja-patra*, *tvak* or *dalchini* (cinnamon), *lavaṅga* (clove), *candana*, *jātī-patrī, jātī-phala, marica* (black pepper), rose-flower, lotus flower, *aśvagandhā*, *soma-latā, punarnavā, vāsā, citraka, amṛtā, bhūmyāmalakī, rohiṣa* (*agiya ghas*), flower of *banaphśā* (wild violet), *brāhmī*, *śaṅkha-puṣpī, tulasī* (holy basil), *pippalī* (long pepper of small size), *śveta candana, cavya, śuṇṭhī* (dry ginger), *musta, miśreyā* (*saunf*), *arjuna,* etc.

Therapeutic Uses :

(1) An Ayurvedic drink, free from alcohol, having sweet taste & the best substitute for tea.

(2) Promotes immunity in the body, so protects the attack of *kaphaja* diseases; if by somehow there is an attack of *kaphaja* disease, patient gets immediate relief by its use.

(3) Stimulates power of digestion; strengthens body & brain, tranquilizes the brain; controls cholesterol & protects from heart-diseases.

(4) This celestial drink strengthens the liver. The best quality of this drink is that it doesn't harm the unctuousness of milk, & is absolutely free from nicotine. On the other hand, there are different varieties of tea which are available in the market,

contain nicotine, & those cause different types of complications like gas, constipation & hyper-acidity.

Mode of Administration : Prepare like common tea; boil more than common tea, more boiling gives more effects of herbs added in the preparation; add sugar according to the taste.

Dosage : Like a common tea, as per requirement. Add the powder equal or lesser than common tea.

(13) *DIVYA* DHĀRĀ

Main Ingredients : Pepper mint, *karpūra*, extract of *ajamodā* (*ajavayan*), clove oil.

Therapeutic Uses : Cures cholera, headace, toothache, ear-diseases, epistaxis, trauma, urticaria, coughing, indigestion, suppression of the power of digestion, colic pain, gas, flatulence and asthma (dyspnoea).

Mode of Administration & Dosage :

i) **Cholera :** 5-10 drops, after every 15 minutes. As patient feels relief in the attack of disease, the period of interval should be increased gradually, i.e. half an hour, one hour, then two hours and so on, it gives definite relief in cholera.

ii) **Colic pain, Gas, Flatulence & Asthma :** Pour 3-4 drops in sugar, *Batāśā* or in warm water, and take internally.

iii) **Asthma or Dyspnoea :** It gives relief through inhalation (smelling) & by applying on the chest. If the patient is not able to inhale because of severe attack of asthma, then 4-5 drops of this '*Divya-dhārā*' should be added in 1/2 -1 ltr. of boiled water, & give steam to the patient. It gives immediate relief.

iv) **Headache :** Apply 3-4 drops on the forehead & give massage; inhale or smell 1-2 drops, which gives immediate refief.

v) **Toothache :** Dip the cotton in *Divya-dhārā* & keep it on affected tooth.

(14) *DIVYA* DANTA MAÑJANA

Main Ingredients : *Babbūla*, neem, *bakula* (*maulasiri*), *tumburu*, *māyāphala* (*majuphal*), *pippalī* (of small size), root of *ākārakarabha* (*akarakara*), *lavaṅga*, black-salt, cuttle fish, rock-salt, *sphaṭika-bhasma*, *karpūra* or camphor (native), pepper-mint, etc.

Therapeutic Uses :

(1) Strengthens the gums, as a result of which discharge of pus mixed with blood gets stopped;

(2) Takes out the food-particles from teeth;

(3) Removes foul smell of the mouth,

(4) Makes salivary gland fit for doing its work properly; and

(5) Makes teeth healthy & shining.

Mode of Administration : Massage or rub this tooth powder on both, gums & teeth either with the help of middle finger or toothbrush. After that, mouth should be cleaned properly with water. Use twice - in the morning as well as at night after dinner. Administration of this tooth powder cures all types of complaints related to teeth.

(15) *DIVYA* PĪḌĀNTAKA RASA

Main Ingredients : *Ajamodā* (*ajavayan*), *nirguṇḍī, śobhāñjana* (sweet var.), *aśvagandhā, rāsnā, musta, Mahā-Vāta-Vidhvaṃsana Rasa, Pravāla piṣṭī, śilājatu* (mineral pitch), *motī-piṣṭī, kupīlu* (pure), *Hīraka bhasma, daśa-mūla, amṛtā, Yogrāja guggulu, Maṇḍūra bhasma, svarṇa-mākṣika bhasma,* etc.

Therapeutic Uses : Useful in joint pain, arthritis, lumbar pain, cervical spondylitis, sciatica; gives immediate & permanent relief in all types of bodily pains.

Mode of Administration : Take after food with warm milk or warm water.

Dosage : 1-2 tabs., twice a day.

(16) *DIVYA* PĪḌĀNTAKA KVĀTHA

Main Ingredients : Root of *Pippalī* (long pepper), *nirguṇḍī, aśvagandhā, rāsnā, musta* (*nagar motha*), root of *eraṇḍa, śuṇṭhī* or dry ginger, *ajamodā* (*ajavayan*), *gaja pippalī, pārijātaka* and other *vāta*-alleviating ingredients.

Therapeutic Uses : Useful in joint pain, sciatica, all types of pains like arthritis, osteo-arthritis, gout, rheumatoid arthritis, muscular & skeletal pains as well as oedema.

Mode of Administration : Boil 5-10 gms.. of *kvātha* (dry decoction) by adding 400 ml. of water till it remains i.e. 100 ml. & then strain it out. To be taken on empty stomach in the morning & at bed time.

For more & special benefit : Take any *vāyu*-alleviating medicine along with this decoction.

For severe pain & oedema : Use this decoction for bath & fomentation.

Method of Steam Bath with this *Kvātha* :

(1) For taking steam bath, boil this medicine by adding 1-1½ l. of water in a pressure cooker. When steam is prepared, remove the weight (whistle) & fit a rubber pipe (used for gas stove) on that place. Now steam will come out from the other side of the pipe, which should be used for affected part of the body. Care should be taken & body should be protected from the direct hot water sprinkles coming out from steam. So a piece of cloth should be tied on that side of pipe. After taking steam, remaining water may be used for fomentation by pouring moderate hot decoction on painful part.

(2) If one doesn't want to steam the affected part, he may foment in another way. For this, boil the medicine in 3-4 ltrs. of water till half of it remains. Then soak a piece of cloth in this moderately warm water, and affected part of the body should be fomented with the help of this cloth.

(17) *DIVYA* PĪḌĀNTAKA TAILA

Main Ingredients : *Vatsanābha, madhu-yaṣṭī,* root of *pippalī* (long pepper), rock-salt, *vaca, gaja-pippalī, jaṭā-māṃsī, nāga-keśara, haridrā, dāru-haridrā, teja-patra, bhṛṅga-rāja, mañjiṣṭhā,* root of *palāśa, puṣkara-mūla, sugandha-bālā, śatāvarī, śuṇṭhī* (dry ginger), seed of *śata-puṣpā*, root of *citraka, miśreyā* (*saunf*), root of *eraṇḍa*, root of *arka, dhattūra, ajamodā* (*ajavayan*), *kupīlu, jyotiṣmatī* (*mal-kangani*), *gandha-prasāraṇī, rāsnā, nirguṇḍī, laśuna*, cow's milk, curd (yoghurt), *daśa-mūla, jīvaka, medā, vṛddhi, kākolī, kṣīra-kākolī*, sesame oil, etc.

Therapeutic Uses : Relieves immediately joint pain, pain of lumbar region and knee-joints, cervical spondylitis, slip disk, trauma & different types of pain, oedema & inflammation.

Mode of Administration : Only for external use; massage should be done gently. Always do gentle massage towards heart by putting moderate pressure.

(18) *DIVYA* YAUVANĀMṚTA VAṬĪ

Main Ingredients : *Jatī-patrī, jātī-phala, keśara, jūnda bedastara, svarṇa-bhasma*, seed of *ātma-guptā* (*kaunch*), *ākāra-karabha* (*akarakara*), seed of *balā*, *śatāvara, Makaradhvaja,* etc.

Therapeutic Uses :

(1) Exceedingly strength promoting & nourishing for persons whose body is exhausted & emaciated; and also useful for persons who are entering into old age;

(2) Strengthens heart & brain, promotes sexual desire, and makes the body active. It is an aphrodisiac;

(3) The best spermatogenetic, strength promoting, nourishing, aphrodisiac, promoter of *ojas* (vital essence), *tejas* (splendour) luster & youthness as well as curative of impotency.

Mode of Administration : To be taken in the morning and in the evening or at night with hot milk.

Dosage : 1 tab., twice a day.

(19) *DIVYA* MADHUNĀŚINĪ VAṬĪ

Main Ingredients : Extracts of *amṛtā, jambū* (black berry), *kaṭukī, nimba, kirāta tiktaka* (*chirayata*), *guḍamāra, kāravellaka* (bitter gourd), *kuṭaja, go-kṣura, karcūra, haridrā, kāla-megha*, fruit of *babbūla, kṛṣṇa jīraka, ativiṣā* (pungent var.), *aśvagandhā, bilva, triphalā* (a collective name for *harītakī, bibhītakī* & *āmalakī*) and adventitious roots of *vaṭa, śilājatu, methikā,* etc.

Therapeutic Uses :

(1) Activates pancreas and helps it ot secrete balanced quantity of Insulin, through which extra Glucose gets converted into Glycogen.

(2) Removes weakness & irritation, as well as increases the capacity of brain by making it strong.

(3) Cures thenumbnessof hands & feet and makes the nervous system strong.

(4) Removes the complications like exhaustion, weakness & tension caused by diabetes.

(5) Protects the patient from morbid thirst, frequent urination, loss of weight, blurred of vision, tingling sensation tiredness, infections of skin, gums & urethera.

(6) Strengthens immune system & increases hope as well as self confidence.

Mode of Administration :

i) Take it one hour before breakfast and dinner or after breakfast and dinner with luke warm water or milk.

ii) If patient takes insulin or allopathic medicine, then he should the get examined the level of his blood–sugar two weeks after the intake of this medicine i.e. *'Madhu-nāśinī'*. As the level of sugar becomes normal, the dose of allopathic medicine should be reduced gradually.

iii) After the stoppage of allopathic medicine, as the level of blood sugar is reduced and becomes normal, the dose of *'Madhunāśinī'* should also reduced gradually.

Dosage : 1 - 2 tabs., twice a day.

(20) *DIVYA* MADHUKALPA VAṬĪ

Main Ingredients : Same ingredients as used in *Madhunāśinī* in fine powder form (not the extracts). Powders of all these ingredients are mixed of made to tablest.

Therapeutic Uses : Same as mentioned in *'Madhunāśinī'* (medicine no. 19).

Mode of Administration : Same as mentioned in *'Madhunaśinī'*.

(21) *DIVYA* MUKTĀ VAṬĪ

Main Ingredients : A celestial medicine prepared with pious herbs found in Himalayas, like *brāhmī, śaṅkha-puṣpī, ustūkhūdūsa* (Arabian or French Lavender), *arjuna, puṣkara-mūla, jaṭā-māṃsī, sarpa-gandhā, jyotiṣmatī, vacā, aśvagandhā* and other cooling drugs like *motī-piṣṭī* (*muktā piṣṭī*).

Therapeutic Uses :

1. Absolutely free from side effects.

2. Cures high blood pressure caused by any reason either by kidney-disorder or by heart disease or by increased cholestrol, anxiety, tension or by hereditary reasons.
3. Also cures associated complications like insomnia feeling of uneasiness, palpitation, pain in the chest head, there is no need to take any extra medicine for the reaiey of these comlecations. Intake of this '*Muktā Vaṭī*' doesn't produce excessive sleep in presons who already have normal sleep.
4. there is no nee to take allopathic or any other medicine along with the administratin of '*Muktā Vaṭī*' : if a patient already takes any other medicine he may stop that undoubtedly. It any patient has been taking other medicine for a long time, and is habitual of taking that medicine is doubtjul , then first he should gradually reduce the dose of that medicine along with the intake of '*Muktā Vaṭī*'. Thereafter, he stop that former medicine gradually.
5 *Muktā Vaṭī* also gives immediate realief to those patients blood pressure doesn't become normal even by the intake of allopathic medicine who are suffering from inssomina (sleeplessness) as well as uneasiness.
6 Allopathic medicines give only temporarily reliey, as there are not able to root out the disease, whereas '*Muktā Vaṭī*' cures the disease for ever within the short period of one or one a half year. It normaliges the blood pressure and there is no need to take any type of medicine.
7 If edxceptionally one has to take '*Muktā Vaṭī*' for a long time even then there is no harm as it doesn't produce any side effect.

Mode of Administration & Dosage :

i) **If B.P. is 160/100 mmhg. Or more while taking allopathich med. :** 2 –2 tabs. Thrice a day – before breakfast, before lunch on hour debore diner with gresh normal water.

ii) **If B.P. is 140/90 mmhg. while taking allopathic med. :** 2 –2 tabs twice a day – before breakfast diner.

iii) It will be more effective if tab is chewed first and then water is taken. Allopathic medicine should be stopped when B.P. becomes normal.

Note : If patient is taking allopathic med. then he should be made to check his B.P. after starting '*Muktā Vaṭī*'. When B.P. becomes normal even without taking allopathic med. then allopathic medicine should be discontinued. If patent is habitual of taking allopathic medicine for a long time, then the dosage should be reduced gradually and then stopped. Meanwhile 2 tabs. of '*Muktā Vaṭī*' (after breakfast or lunch) should be continued. If by taking '*Muktā Vaṭī*' (2 tabs.) once a day, B.P. becomes normal for some period, then dosage should be reduced to one tab. per day in the morning. This wil stablize B.P. in the normal level. Dose of one tab. (once a day). should be continued for some days. Then B.P. will be come 120/80 mmhg. or lesser. Now the dose of '*Muktā Vaṭī*' should be reduced to one tab. twice a week, and then one tab once a week. Thereafter intak, of the medicine should be stopped. Now B.P. will remain normal and the patient will be healthy and fit.

Prescriptions :

1. Take light and digestive food;
2. Take 2 to 4 tumblers of water early in the morning.

Prohibitions : Take salt in less quantity. In the place of sea-salt, rock-salt should be taken.

(22) *DIVYA* MEDHĀ KVĀTHA

Main Ingradients : *Brāhmī* , *śaṅkha-puṣpī, aśvagandhā, jaṭā māṃsī, ustūkhūdūsa* (Arabian or French lavender), *jyotiṣmatī* (*malkangani*), *miśreyā* (*saunf*), *gojihvā* (*gājaban*), etc.

Therapeutic Uses :

1. Cures chronic headache, migraine, sleeplessness or less of sleep, negativity and depression,
2. Cures uneasiness;
3. Promotes memory.

Mode of Administration : Prepare decoction according to the procedure. (Boil 5 – 10 gm. of medicine by adding 400 ml. of water till it is reduced to 100 ml. and strain it out) and take twice a day in the morning and evening.

Produces better and instantaneous effect if *Medhā vaṭī* is also taken with this decoction.

(23) *DIVYA* MEDHĀ VAṬĪ

Main Ingredients : Extracts of *brāhmī, śaṅkha-puṣpī, vacā, jyotiṣmatī, aśvagandhā, jaṭā māṃsī, ustūkhūdūsa* (Arabian or French Lavender), *puṣkara-mūla,* etc. and *pravāla piṣṭī, motī* (*muktā*) *piṣṭī, rajata bhasma,* etc.

Therapeutic Uses :

(1) Cures different types of mental disorders, like loss of memory, headache, insomnia, irritative temperament, epileptic fits;

(2) Cools down the brain;

(3) Cures excessive dreams, depression due to negative thinking, and uneastness;

(4) Very useful in loss of memory in old persons and forgetting anything all of sudden, but doesn't produce any side effect;

(5) Promotes self confidence and enthusiasm;

(6) Very useful & beneficial for students & intellectuals; it is best mental; tonic; should be used regularly for promoting memory & wisdom;

Mode of Administration : To be taken on empty stomach with milk or after breakfast with water, & in the evening after dinner with water/ milk.

Dosage : 1-2 tabs, twice daily.

(24) *DIVYA* AMṚTA RASĀYANA (LINCTUS)

Main Ingredients : Paste of *āmalakī,* cow's ghee, *keśara, brāhmī, śaṅkha-puṣpī*, almond, *vaṃśa-locana, elā, tvak* (cinnamon), *śatāvārī*, seed of *kapi-kacchū, pravāla piṣṭī,* etc.

Therapeutic Uses :

(1) Excedingly useful rejuvenating that gives full nourishment to the brain, wisdom promoting, cooling & promoter of strength, nourishment as well as health of the whole body.

(2) Nourishes the body, promotes lustre & useful for eyes.

(3) Cooling & rejuvenating which is to be particularly administered in summer reason.

(4) An excellent tonic for students & intellectuals as well.

Mode of Administration : To be taken with milk or with meals as pickle in the morning & evening.

Dosage : 1-2 teaspoonfuls (10 gm. - 20gm.) twice a day.

(25) *DIVYA* MEDOHARA VAṬĪ (WEIGHTLESS)

Main Ingredients : Pure *guggulu, śilājīta sat* (extract of mineral pitch), solid extracts of *harītakī* or *harad*, *bibhītaka* or *baheda*, *āmalakī, kaṭukī*, root of *punarnavā, trivṛt* or *nishoth*, *viḍaṅga,* etc.

Therapeutic Uses :

(1) First removes the disorders of digestive system and then reduces the extra fat & makes the body beautiful, compact, lustreful & active.

(2) Especially useful in thyroid disorders (hypo & hyper thyroid), rheumatic arthritis, joint pains, pain in lumbar region and knee. joints.

(3) Digests the *medas* (fat) in the body & nourishes the successive tissue elements viz. bone, bone-marrow & *śukra* (semen). In other words, it converts the fat into other tissue elements as a results of which body becomes healthy & compact, it doesn't produce any adverse effect.

Mode of Administration : Half an hour before meals or one hour after meals with hot water.

Dosage : 1-2 tabs. twice or thrice a day, according to the weight of the body.

Precautions :

Avoid :

(1) Sweet things & ghee (clarified butter); and

(2) Fried food, food prepared with fine-flour (*maida*) & things which promote fat.

Take : Hot water early in the morning as well as for drinking.

(26) *DIVYA* ŚVĀSĀRI RASA

Main Ingredients : *Pravāla piṣṭī, Abhraka bhasma, muktā-śukti bhasma, ṭaṅkaṇa bhasma, sphaṭika bhasma, godantī bhasma, kapardaka bhasma, śṛṅga bhasma, manaḥśilā* (pure), root of *ākāra-karabha, lavaṅga* (clove), *tvak* (cinnamon), pure *vatsanābha*, powder of *trikaṭu* (collective name for *śuṇṭhī* or dry ginger, *pippalī* or long pepper and *marica* or black papper), *karkaṭa śṛṅgī, madhu yaṣṭī,* fruit of *rudantī,* etc.

Therapeutic Uses :

(1) Intake of this medicine makes the cells of lungs more active, and removes the inflammation of bronchioles & bronchi. So lungs become capable to take more oxygen & patient gets rid of chronic diseases like bronchitis;

(2) An expectorant by the intake of which phlegm adhered in lungs comes out easily and there is no further formation of phlegm;

(3) Promotes the immune power of lungs, nad cures cough, coryza, cold, asthma, sneezing, heaviness in the head and sinusitis;
(4) An excellent tonic for lungs to nourish them.

Mode of Administration : To be taken half an hour before meals with honey or warm water, can be taken after meals also.

Dosage : 500 mg. to 1 gm., twice of thrice a day.

Note : If there is severe attack of dyspnoea, then following medicines should be added to 50 gm. of *Śvāsāri Rasa* :

Śṛṅga bhasma	:	10 gm.
Abhraka bhasma	:	10 gm.
Pravāla piṣṭī	:	10 gm.

This will be more effective and give quicker relief.

(27) *DIVYA* STRĪ RASĀYANA VAṬĪ

Main Ingredients : *Putrañjīvaka, śveta candana, kamala, dāru-haridrā, vaṃśa-locana, Parvāla piṣṭī, śilājatu* (mineral pitch), *śatāvarī*, seeds of *śivaliṅgī, pārasa pīpala, madhu-yaṣṭī, triphalā* (collective name for *harītakī, bibhītakī* & *āmalakī*), *ambara-dhāna, bījabanda (*seeds of *balā), āmalaka, aśoka, Mayūra-piccha bhasma, nāga keśara, aśvagandhā, deva-dāru, guggulu* (pure), etc.

Therapeutic Uses :

(1) Cures all types of diseases of woman viz., leucorrhoea, menorrhagia, irregularity in menstruation, pain in lower abdomen or lumbar region;
(2) Very useful in excessive bleeding during menstruation; cures all types of female-diseases if taken regularly for some time;
(3) Useful in curing wrinkles on the face, dark circles below eyes, feeling of exhaustion in the body & laziness.

Mode of Administration : To be taken after food with milk/water.

Dosage : 1-2 tabs., twice or thrice a day.

(28) *DIVYA* HṚDAYĀMṚTA VAṬĪ

Main Ingredients : Extracts from bark of *arjuna, amṛtā, aśvagandhā, rāsnā, nirguṇḍī, punarnavā, citraka, musta* (*nagar motha*), *Hīraka bhasma, Śṛṅga bhasma, Akīka piṣṭī, Saṅge yaśada piṣṭī, Muktā - piṣṭī, Rajata bhasma, śilājīta sat, guggulu* (pure), etc.

Therapeutic Uses :

(1) Strengthens the heart, removes the blockage of the arteries of heart & controls the increased cholesterol;

(2) Instantaneously relieves the frequent occurrence of angina pain;

(3) Activates the inactive capillaries of the heart; promotes its work-capacity, and removes uneasiness & palpitation;

(4) Exceedingly helpful in keeping the heart healthy after removing the blockages of heart;

(5) Also useful after the surgery of heart to keep it normal & healthy.

Mode of Administration : To be taken in the morning & evening with luke- warm milk/water or the decoction of the bark of *arjuna.*

Dosage : 1-2 tabs. twice a day.

Method of Preparation of Arjuna-bark Drink : Boil 2-3gm. (1/2 teaspoon approx.) of the *arjuna*-bark with one cup of milk and one cup of water till one cup remains, and then strain out. Alternatively, *arjuna*-bark can be boiled only by adding two cups of water, i.e. without milk.

Note : If a patient is taking allopathic medicines, he should reduce the dose gradually under the supervision of his doctor, as he feels better after the intake of *Hṛdayāmṛta.*

(29) *DIVYA* VĀTĀRI CŪRṆA

Main Ingredients : *Śuṇṭhī* (dry ginger), *aśvagandhā, śobhāñjana* (sweet var.), *kuṭakī, methī,* etc.

Therapeutic Uses :

1. Very useful in all types of *vāta-roga* (diseases caused by the aggravation of *vāyu-doṣa* (and *āma-vāta)* rheumatoid arthritis in which *vāyu* gets agaravated due to the accumulation of *āma* or indigested product caused by the impaired digestion as well as metabolism, and causes pain in the joints of body); and
2. It is anodyne and it cures *āma-vāta* (rheumatoid arthritis), sciatica, pain in back as well as in lumbar region.

Mode of Administration : Take after food with hot water or milk.
Dosage : 2-4 gms. twice a day.

(30) *DIVYA* ŚILĀJĪTA RASĀYANA VAṬĪ

Main Ingredients : *Śilājatu, aśvagandhā, bhūmyāmalakī* or *bhumi amala, triphalā* (collective name for *harītakī, bibhītakī* & *āmalaka*), etc.

Therapeutic Uses :

1. Produces positive effect on *vātavahinī nāḍī* (nervous system), kidneys and channels which carry *vīrya* (semen);
2. *Vayu*-alleviating, promoter of strength and the quantity of semen (spermatopoetic);
3. Particularly useful in night fall *svapnadoṣa, prameha* (obstinate urinary disorders including diabetes) and leucorrhoea.

Mode of Administration : To be taken after food with luke-warm milk / water.

Dosage : 2 tabs. twice a day.

(31) *DIVYA* SARVA-KALPA KVĀTHA

Main Ingredients : *Punarnavā, bhūmyāmalakī, āragvadha* (*amaltas*), *kāka-mācī* (*makoy*), etc.

Therapeutic Uses :

1. By the intake of this decoction liver gets stimulated as a result of which liver start doing its work perfectly;
2. Because of the intake of polluted or packed food, polluted drinks (soft drinks, cold drinks, tea, coffee, etc.), different types of poisonous chemicals get accumulated inside of our body which results in the sluggishness (inactivity) of the liver. It gives rise to different types of diseases including jaundice. As jaundice becomes chronic, it converts into incurable stage like hepatitis B & C. This *Sarva-kalpa Kvātha* activates the liver and makes it healthy after curing the chronic stages of hepatitis B & C.
3. Cures jaundice, enlargement and sweling of liver, oedema, oliguria, oedema all over the body, pain in the stomach and lower abdomen, indigestion of food and loss of appetite.

Mode of Administratin : Boil one teaspoonful (5gm. approx.) of this *kvātha* with one tumbler (300 ml. approx.) of water till one fourth of its remains. After straining out it should be taken on empty stomach in the morning one hour before dinner or at bed time. If patient is suffering from constipation then 8–10 *munakkās* (raisins) should be added while boiling.

(32) *DIVYA* KĀNTI LEPA

Main Ingredients : Seeds & leaves of *madayantikā* (henna), *āmra gandhi haridrā* (*amba haldi*), *haridrā* (turmeric), *mañjiṣṭhā, jātī-phala, śveta candana, tagara* (*sugandha bālā*), *sphaṭika bhasma, samudra phena* (cuttle fish), *khadira, karpūra,* etc.

Therapeutic Uses :

(1) Instantaneously cures skin-disorders, viz. pimples, acne, wrinkles on face, loss of shining & luster, darkness, etc.;

(2) Application of this paste absorbs all the complaints of skin , as a result of which skin again becomes healthy; natural beauty of face reappears; it also promotes splendour, shining & luster on the face.

Mode of Administration : Take one teaspoonful of this powder, make a paste by adding either rose-water or unboiled milk, then apply on the face, allow it to remain for 3-4 hours and wash the face with luke-warm water.

***

CHAPTER - II
CLASSICAL MEDICINES

(1) *DIVYA* ŚILĀJĪTA SAT

Source of Main Ingredient : A celestial exudation (resin) which trickles out from high Himalayan range, it naturally contains fine mixture of seven metals like gold, silver, iron, etc.

Therapentic Uses : In the praise of *śilājīta* (bitumen), it is said in the classic ***"Na so'sti rogo bhuvi sādhya-rūpaḥ śilāhvyam yanna jayet prasahyah "***

There is no disease (caused by the vitiation of *rasa-dhātu*) in this world which does not get cured by the administration of *śilājatu* (bitumen) . It is an excellent rejuvenator to make the body healthy (free from diseases) & firm. After curing the different types of chronic & painful diseases, obesity, dibetes mellitus & weakness caused by it, *śilājīta* makes the body strong & lustrous.

(1) Cures gout , cervical spondylitis, sciatica, pain in lumbar region & knee joints, parkinsonism, joint pain & all other types of pain;

(2) Very effective remedy for cold, cough, rhinitis, coryza, asthma (dyspnoea), bronchitis, weakness of lungs , tuberculosis, weakness of bones, general weakness, seminal diseases , diabetes, etc.,

(3) Promotes immunity power , can be taken by all i.e men, women even by children to cure diseases.

Mode of Administration & Dosage : *Śilājīta* available in the Trust (*Divya Yog Mandir*) is absolutely pure , so it is very effective. Its dosage is prescribed as follows :

(1) **In summer season :** Equal to one moong seed, twice a day.

(2) **In winter :** Equal to 1-2 gms., twice a day.

(3) **In general :** 1-2 drops, twice a day.

(4) To be taken with hot milk. People who do not take milk, they can take along with hot water also.

(2) *DIVYA* MUKTĀ PIṢṬĪ (Āyurveda Sāra Saṅgraha)

Therapeutic Uses :

(1) Cures *rakta-pitta* (bleeding from various parts of the body), weakness, headache, aggravation of *pitta*, burning sensation, *prameha* (obstinate urinary diseases including diabetes) and *mūtra-kṛcchra* (dysuria). It is cold in potency.

(2) Instantneously cures aggravation of *pitta*, acidity, burning sensation in urethera & all over the body , insomnia, harshness in speech, irritation, increased heat (warmth) in the brain , aversion from food; particularly useful in increased heart-beat (palpitation) & insomnia (sleeplessness) . Also useful in giddiness caused by stroke of brain-veins due to excessive anger, excessive awakeness, excessive reading exposure to the sun & excessive intake of *paittika* food ingredients (*pitta*-aggravating ingredients).

(3) Exceedingly beneficial in bleeding from nose , mouth & rectum due to the exposure to strong sun or fire during summer, burning sensation in head, eyes & all over the body as well as uneasiness.

(4) Relieves complication (like burning syndrome, morbid thirst, fever, uncomfort, etc.) associated with consumption caused by aggravated *pitta*, & burning in throat as well as sour eructations due to hyper-acidity .

Mode of Administration & Dosage : 1-4 *rattīs* (125mg.-500mg.), twice a day on empty stomach along with butter, milk-cream, honey, *Cyavana prāśa, gulkanda, Āmalā murbbā* or *Brāhmī śarbata.*

(3) *DIVYA* SVARṆA BHASMA (Rasa Taraṅgiṇī)

Therapeutic Uses :

1. Gold (*svarṇa*) is the best amongst metals . *Bhasma* (calcined powder) prepared with this metal i.e. *Svarṇa-bhasma* is also exceedingly useful to cure psycho-somatic diseases. It produces miraculous effect in almost all diseases, but some diseases like tuberculosis does not get cured without this medicine.
2. Medicines prepared by adding *svarṇa-bhasma* cure poisonous diseases , weakness , *dhātu-kṣaya* (diminution of tissue elements),

chronic arthritis , kala-azar and malaria . It also cures the patients who are very emaciated and who do not get cured otherwise.

3. Though *Svarṇa-bhasma* is powerful, it is non-evacing substance. It purifies the vitiated (polluted) blood, nourishes the heart & makes the brain, mind, nervous system, kidney & other bodily organs active resulting in the promotion of splendour & luster of the body . It originates new spirit (vitality) in the body & enthusiasm in the mind.
4. After promoting the immunity power in the body, this *bhasma* destroys the heterogenous substances therein.

(4) *DIVYA* CYAVANA PRĀŚA (Bhaiṣajya Ratnāvatī)

Therapeutic Uses :

1. *Cyavana prāśa* is useful not only for patients but also is an excellent rejuvenator (tonic) for healthy persons.
2. It removes physical & mental weakness caused by any reason, strengthens lungs as well as heart. After curing cough, phlegm and bronchitis, it makes the body nourished & compact.
3. After nourishing the seven *dhātus* of the body (tissue elements, viz.(1) *rasa* or chyle including lymph, (2) *rakta* or the haemoglobin fraction of the blood, (3) *māṃsa* or muscle tissue, (4) *medas* or fat tissue, (5) *asthi* or bone tissue, (6) *majjā* or bone-marrow, and (7) *śukra* or the sperm in male & ovum in female, it promotes strength, virility, energy, lustre & intellect.
4. People of all age-groups and genders including children women & old persons, can take this medicine equally.

Mode of Administration : Twice on empty stomach, milk should be taken after half an hour.

Dosage : 1-2 teaspoonfuls (1.5-2.5 *tolās* or 15gm.-25gm;), twice a day.

(5) *DIVYA* CANDRAPRABHĀ VAṬĪ (Bhaiṣajya Ratnāvalī)

Therapeutic Uses :

1. Very famous & useful medicine for the diseases of urinary organs & uterus as well as seminal disorders.
2. Cures *mūtra-kṛcchra* (dysuria) caused by prostate enlargement, suppression of urination, joint pains, arthritis, cervical sciatica, weakness, stone in urinary tract, all types of *prameha* (obstinate

urinary diseases including diabetes), *bhagandara* (fistula-in-ano), testicle enlargement, anemia, *kāmalā* (serious type of jaundice), piles & lumbar pain; promotes fluid and nourishment in the body.

3. Promotes strength, nourishment & lustre, produces gradual & permanent effect in *prameha* (obstinate urinary disorders including diabetes) & complication arising out of it; cures seminal disorders caused by gonorrhoea and syphilis.
4. Bring about lustre in men & women who have become lustreless due to excessive seminal discharge & menstruation respectively.
5. Nourishes tissue elements (*rasa, rakta* etc.) in the patients suffering from weakness (emaciation) & paleness of body, suppression of the power of digestion, dyspnoea caused by little exertion shrunken eyes & anorexia (loss of appetite); alleviates *vāyu* and makes the body lustrous as well as splenderous after nourishing it.

Mode of Administration : To be taken with hot water/milk or with any other medicine according to the requirement of the patient.

Dosage : 2-4 tabs., twice or thrice a day.

(6) *DIVYA* VASANTA KUSUMĀKARA RASA (Bhaiṣajya Ratnāvalī)

Theraputic Uses :

1. A marvellous excellent rejuvenator which is energetic & cardiac tonic; & which cures excessive urination, all types of *prameha* (obstinate urinary disorders including diabetes), *soma-roga* (diseases of female genital organ), leucorrhoea, disorders related to female genital organs and uterus, thinness of semen, premature ejaculation of semen as well as other complaints related to semen. It is a costly medicine for curing wasting caused by the diminution of semen.
2. Cures weakness of heart, lungs & brain, colic pain, *rakta-pitta* (bleeding from diffrent parts of body), cough, bronchitis, dyspnoea (asthma), sprue syndrome, menorrhagia, leucorrhoea, anemia and weakness in old age after curing the disease.
3. Very famous medicine for diabetes mellitus.

Mode of Administration : To be taken along with butter, milk-cream, honey or milk on empty stomach in the morning & evening.

Dosage : 2-4 *rattīs* (250mg.-500mg.), twice daily.

(7) *DIVYA* BĀDĀMA PĀKA

(Rasa-taraṅgiṇī Sāra & Siddha Prayoga-saṅgraha)

Therapeutic Uses :

1. Nourishing rejuvenating which cures mental and cardiac weakness, diseases caused by aggravation of *pitta*, & eye-disease.
2. A miraculous medicine for headache; should be taken regularly by intellectuals.
3. Nourishes the body; promotes strength, semen & splendour; and is very useful in sterility, *dhvaja-bhaṅga* (atonic condition of the phallus) & nervous weakness.

Mode of Administration : To be taken in the morning & evening with cow's milk or water.

Dosage : 1-2 *tolās* (10-20gms.), twice daily.

CHAPTER - III
SELF-EXPERIENCED TREATMENT OF SOME DISEASES

INITIAL INSTRUCTIONS & INDICATIONS

Following recipes described according to the diseases are tested through the medicines prepared in '*Divya Yog Mandir* (Trust)' only. These medicines have been prepared in the pharmacy, and tested in the laboratory of the Ashram.

The dose and the mode of administration of particular medicine can be changed according to the nature of disease and the patient. If after the intake of medicine any patient suffers from heating sensation and diarrhoea then the dose should be reduced to half or one-fourth. In the cases of acute, chronic and incurable diseases, it is necessary to consult the physician before starting the medicine.

[For the attainment of full benefit (as mentioned), intake of medicine as well as regular practice of *Yog* & *Prāṇāyāma* (breathing exercise) prescribed by honourable Swami Ramdevji should be performed simultaneously which is very essential.]

(1) OBESITY

1. ***DIVYA* MEDOHARA VAṬĪ (Weightless)**

Dose : 1-2 tabs., twice a day.

Mode of Administration : Take half an hour before or after the breakfast & dinner.

Anupāna : Luke-warm water.

Note : Patient suffering from constipatoin should take 1 teaspoonful (5gms.) of *triphalā cūrṇa* (powder) regularly at bed time with warm water.

(2) MADHUMEHA (DIABETES MELLITUS)

1. ***DIVYA* MADHUNĀŚINĪ VAṬĪ :**

Dose : 2-2 tabs., twice or thrice a day.

Mode of Administration : Take half an hour either before or after the breakfast, lunch & dinner with water / milk.

Note : Be careful and regular about *Prāṇāyāma* (breathing exercise) & *pathya* (diet & regimens which are to be taken or avoided).

[**For details :** See description on '*Divya Madhunāśinī Vaṭī*', ref. : Ch.-I, Page no. 19]

2. ***DIVYA* ŚILĀJĪTA :**

Dose : 1-1drop, twice a day.

Mode of Administration : To be taken in the morning & evening on empty stomach with warm milk.

(3) HIGH BLOOD PRESSURE (UCCA-RAKTA-CĀPA)

1. ***DIVYA* MUKTĀ VAṬĪ :**

Dose : 1-2 tabs., twice a day.

Mode of Administration : To be taken in the morning on empty stomach and in the evening half an hour before dinner with water.

[**For details :** See description on '*Divya Muktā Vaṭī*', ref. : Ch. I, Page no. 11]

(4) PIMPLES OR ACNE VULGARIS (YUVĀNA PĪḌIKĀ)

1. ***DIVYA*** **KĀYĀ-KALPA VAṬĪ :**

Dose : 2-2 tabs., twice a day.

Mode of Administration : To be taken in the morning one hour before breakfast and in the evening one hour before dinner with water.

2. ***KHADIRĀRIṢṬA*** **:**

Dose : 4 teaspoonful, twice a day.

Mode of Administration : To be taken after lunch (or breakfast) & dinner by adding 4 teaspoons of water.

3. ***DIVYA*** **KĀNTI LEPA :**

Quantity : as required.

Mode of Administration : Make a paste by adding rose-water, un-boiled milk or water; apply on the face & wash with luke-warm water after two or three hours; alternatively can be applied at night & washed in the morning

Note : Patient who suffers from constipation should take any laxative, e.g *Triphalā* powder, *'Udara-kalpa cūrṇa'* or *'Divya cūrṇa'* regularly.

(5) LEUCODERMA (ŚVETA KUṢṬHA)

(A)	**1.** ***DIVYA*** **KĀYĀ-KALPA** ***VAṬĪ***	**20 gms.**	**Mode of Administration :** Mix all these three medicines together & divide into 90 dosages, take one dose an hour before each meal i.e. breakfast, lunch & dinner with water.
	2. ***DIVYA*** **AMṚTĀ SAT**	**20 gms.**	
	3. ***DIVYA*** **ŚUDDHA** ***BĀVACĪ*** **CŪRṆA**	**50 gms.**	

(B) 2. ***MAHĀ MAÑJIṢṬHĀRIṢṬA*** **:**

Dose : 4 teaspoonfuls twice daily.

Mode of Administration : Take after lunch or breakfast & dinner by adding 4 teaspoons of water.

(C) 3. ***DIVYA*** **ŚVITRAGHNA LEPA :**

Mode of Administration : Prepare a paste by mixing cow's urine & the juice of neem-leaves, then apply on the spots.

Note : Patients to whom paste does not suit and who feel heating & burning sensation after application of this paste, they should avoid this.

(B) 4. *DIVYA* KĀYĀ-KALPA TAILA :

Dose : 1-2 drops, twice a day.

Mode of Administration : To be applied on the at bed time.

(6) OLIGOSPERMIA (DIMINUTION OF SPERMS) & OTHER GENITAL DISEASES

(A) 1. *DIVYA* YAUVANĀMṚTA	**2 tabs.**	**Mode of Administration :** To be taken in the morning after breakfast & in the evening after dinner, with milk.
2. *DIVYA* CANDRAPRABHĀ *VAṬĪ*	**2 tabs.**	

(B) *DIVYA* ŚILĀJĪTA SAT

Dose : 1-2 drops, twice a day.

Mode of Administration : To be mixed with milk & taken with no.1

(7) TUMOUR OR ADENITIS *(GRANTHI)* OR ANY GROWTH OF BODY

1. *DIVYA* KĀÑCANĀRA *GUGGULU*	**2 tabs.**	**Mode of Administration :** Take after lunch (or breakfast) & dinner, with luke –warm water
2. *DIVYA* VṚDDHIVĀDHIKĀ *VAṬĪ*	**2 tabs.**	

(8) SPECIAL TREATMENT FOR ADENITIS OF BIG SIZE

1. *DIVYA* ŚILĀ SINDŪRA	**4 gms.**	**Mode of Administration :** Mix all these five medicines together & divide into 60 parts (doses), take each dose twice daily on empty stomach (i.e before breakfast & dinner) by adding honey.
2. *DIVYA* PRAVĀLA PIṢṬĪ	**10 gms.**	
3. *DIVYA* AMṚTĀ SAT	**20 gms.**	
4. *DIVYA* MUKTĀ-ŚUKTI BHASMA	**5 gms.**	
5. *TĀMRA BHASMA*	**1 gms.**	

(9) THALASSEMEA

1. *DIVYA* KUMĀRA-KALYĀṆA RASA	1-2 gms.	**Mode of Administration :** Mix all these six medicines together, divide into 90 parts & make packets. Take each packet twice daily (in the morning – an hour before breakfast & in the evening – an hour before dinner) by adding honey.
2. *DIVYA* PRAVĀLA PIṢṬĪ	5 gms.	
3. *DIVYA* KAHARAVĀ PIṢṬĪ	5 gms.	
4. *DIVYA* MOTĪ PIṢṬĪ	2 gms.	
5. *DIVYA* AMṚTĀ SAT	10 gms.	
6. *DIVYA* PRAVĀLA PAÑCĀMṚTA	5 gms.	

Note : In addition, intake of the juice of *ghṛta kumārī* (*Aloe vera*), *guḍūcī* (*Tinospora cordifolia*) & wheat-grass on empty stomach (in the morning & evening) is extremely useful.

(10) TREATMENT OF MUSCULAR DISTROPHY & HANDICAPPED CHILDEREN

(A) 1. *DIVYA* EKĀṄGA VĪRA RASA	5 gms.	**Mode of Administration** : Mix all these medicines together, divide into 90 parts, make packets and take each twice on empty stomach (in the morning & evening) with honey.
2. *DIVYA* PRAVĀLA PIṢṬĪ	10 gms.	
3. *DIVYA* AMṚTĀ SAT	10 gms.	
4. *DIVYA* SVARṆA MĀKṢIKA BHASMA	5 gms.	
5. *DIVYA* RASARĀJA RASA	1 gm.	
6. *DIVYA* VASNTA KUSUMĀKARA RASA	1 gm.	
7. *DIVYA* MOTĪ PIṢṬĪ	2 gms.	

(B) 1. *DIVYA* ŚILĀJĪTA RASĀYANA	1 tab.	**Mode of Administration :** Take twice daily with milk.
2. *DIVYA* TRAYODAŚĀṄGA GUGGULU	1 tab.	
3. *DIVYA* CHANDRA-PRABHĀ VAṬĪ	1 tab.	

Note : For children half tab. of each should be given.

(C) 1. *DIVYA* AŚVAGANDHĀ *CŪRṆA*	2gms.	**Mode of Administration :** Take twice or thrice daily after meals i.e. breakfast, lunch and dinner (the first one should be preferably taken with milk & second one should be taken by adding 4 teaspoons of water).
OR *DIVYA* AŚVAGANDHĀRIṢṬĀ	4 teaspoons	

Note : Take the juice of wheat grass + *guḍūcī,* twice on empty stomach.

(11) TREATMENT OF MENTAL RETARDATION & MONGOLOID CHILDREN

(A) 1. *DIVYA* MEDHĀ VAṬĪ – 60 gms.

Dose : 1-2 tabs., twice a day.

Mode of Administration : Take in the morning and evening with milk.

(B) 2. *DIVYA* AŚVAGANDHĀ CŪRṆA –100 gms.

Dose : 2 gms. twice a day

Mode of Administration : Take in the morning and evening with milk along with no.1.

(C) 1. *DIVYA* MOTĪ PIṢṬĪ	5 gms.	**Mode of Administration :** Mix all these four medicines together, divide into sixty parts & take each dose on empty stomach twice daily with honey.
2. *DIVYA* PRAVĀLA PIṢṬĪ	10 gms.	
3. *DIVYA* AMṚTĀ SAT	10 gms,	
4. *DIVYA* RAJATA BHASMA	2 gms.	

(D) 1. *DIVYA* MEDHĀ KVĀTHA : 300 gms.

Mode of Administration : Boil one teaspoon (5 gms.) of this dry *kvātha* by adding one glass (300 ml.) of water till it is reduced to 1/4th, strain it out & take twice on empty stomach in the morning & evening.

(12) MULTIPLE SCLEROSIS

(A)1. *DIVYA* EKĀṄGAVĪRA RASA 5 gms.
2. *DIVYA* MAHĀ VĀTA VIDHVAṂSANA RASA 5 gms.
3. *DIVYA* PRAVĀLA PIṢṬĪ 10 gms.
4. *DIVYA* AMṚTĀ SAT 10 gms.
5. *DIVYA* BṚHAD VĀTA CINTĀMAṆI RASA 1-2 gms.

Mode of Administration: Mix all these five medicines together, divide into sixty doses (parts), make packets & take each twice a day (in the morning & evening) on empty stomach, with honey.

(B) 1. *DIVYA* TRAYODAŚĀṄGA GUGGULU 60 gms.
2. *DIVYA* CANDRA-PRABHĀ VAṬĪ 60 gms.
3. *DIVYA* ŚILĀJĪTA RASĀYANA 60 gms.

Mode of Administration : Take twice a day, after breakfast and lunch, with milk (in the morning) & water (after lunch).

(C) 1. *DIVYA* AŚVAGANDHĀ CŪRṆA - 100 gms. :

Dose : 2 gms.

Mode of Administration : Take twice on empty stomach (in the morning & evening) with milk.

(13) GASTRIC TROUBLE & FLATULENCE

(A) 1. *DIVYA* GAISAHARA CŪRṆA :

Dose : ½ teaspoon, twice or as required.

Mode of Administration : Take after lunch & dinner with warm water.

Note : Can be taken once or twice or more if required.

(B) 2. KUMĀRYĀSAVA :

Dose : 4 teaspoons, twice a day.

Mode of Administration : Take after lunch & dinner by adding 4 teaspoons of water.

(C) 3. *DIVYA* UDARA-KALPA CŪRṆA OR *DIVYA* CŪRṆA :

Dose : 1 teaspoon.

Mode of Administration : To be taken at bed time with hot water, whenever required.

Note : Diabetic patients should not take '*Divya Udara-kalpa Cūrṇa*' as it contains candied sugar, etc.

(14) ĀMA (TOXIC BYPRODUCT), SPRUE SYNDROME & DIARRHOEA

(A)

1. ***DIVYA* GAṄGĀDHARA CŪRṆA**	**50 gms.**	**Dose :** 1 teaspoon, twice a daily. **Mode of Administration :** To be taken one hour before lunch & dinner with water.
2. ***DIVYA* BILVĀDI CŪRṆA**	**50 gms.**	
3. ***DIVYA* ŚAṄKHA BHASMA**	**10 gms.**	
4. ***DIVYA* KAPARDAKA BHASMA**	**10 gms.**	
5. ***DIVYA* MUKTĀ-ŚUKTI BHASMA**	**10 gms.**	

(B)

1. ***DIVYA* KUṬAJAGHANA VAṬĪ**	**40 gms.**	**Dose :** 2–2 tabs. from each, twice a daily. **Mode of Administration :** Take after lunch & dinner along with no. 3.
2. ***DIVYA* CITRAKĀDI VAṬĪ**	**10 gms.**	

(C) *DIVYA* KUṬAJĀRIṢṬA :

Dose : 4 teaspoons, twice daily.

Mode of Administration : Take after lunch & dinner by adding 4 teaspoons of water.

(15) ULCERATIVE COLITIS

(A)

1. **DIYVA MOTĪ PIṢṬĪ**	**5 gms.**	**Mode of Administration :** Mix all these medicines together, divide into 60 parts, make packets, take each packet in the morning & evening on empty stomach with honey.
2. ***DIVYA* ŚAṄKHA BHASMA**	**10 gms.**	
3. ***DIVYA* KAPARDAKA BHASMA**	**10 gms.**	
4. ***DIVYA* MUKTĀ-ŚUKTI BHASMA**	**10 gms.**	

(B) ***DIVYA*** **UDARĀMARṬA :**

Dose : 1 tab. twice a day.

Mode of Administration : Take twice after food with water.

(C) ***DIVYA*** **BELA CŪRṆA :**

Dose : 1 teaspoon, twice a day.

Mode of Administration : Take after food (lunch & dinner) with water.

(D) 4. ***DIVYA*** **SARVA-KALPA KVĀTHA :**

Mode of Administration : Prepare decoction of one teaspoon of this medicine (as prescribed before, see ch.-I, recipe no. 31), and take twice a day i.e. in the morning & evening on empty stomach.

(16) ACIDITY & HYPER ACIDITY

(A) 1. ***DIVYA*** **AVIPATTIKARA CŪRṆA**	**100 gms.**	**Dose :** ½ teaspoon twice daily. **Mode of Administration :** Mix both these medicines together & take half an hour before or after breakfast & dinner.
2. ***DIVYA*** **MUKTĀ-ŚUKTI BHASMA**	**20 gms.**	

IN CHRONIC & HYPER ACIDITY

(B) 1. ***DIVYA*** **MOTĪ PIṢṬĪ**	**4 gms.**	**Mode of Administration :** Mix all these three medicines together, divide into 60 parts, make packets, and take each packet twice / thrice a day, i.e. one hour before breakfast, lunch & dinner either with honey or fresh water.
2. ***DIVYA*** **KĀMADUDHĀ RASA (MUKTĀ YUKTA i.e. with Pearl)**	**20 gms.**	
3. ***DIVYA*** **MUKTĀ-ŚUKTI BHASMA**	**10 gms.**	

Note : If patient is suffering from chronic hyper acidity or many complaints related to it, then he should take both the groups of medicines i.e. A+B. Otherwise, medicines of group 'A' are sufficient to get relief.

Avoid : Intake of brinjal, coconut, ginger, green chilli, garlic, all types of spices, chillies & sharp (hot) as well as fried food articles.

(17) CORONARY ARTERY DISEASE

(A) 1. *DIVYA* MOTĪ PIṢṬĪ	4 gms.	**Mode of Administration :** Mix all these five medicines, divide into 60 parts, make packets & take each packet an hour before breakfast & diner either with honey or warm water.
2. *DIVYA* SAṄGEYAŚADA PIṢṬĪ	5 gms.	
3. *DIVYA* AKĪKA PIṢṬĪ	5 gms.	
4. *DIVYA* ŚṚṄGA BHASMA	10 gms.	
5. *DIVYA* YOGENDRA RASA	1 gm.	

(B) *DIVYA* HṚDAYĀMṚTA – 40 gms.

Dose : 1 – 2 tabs. twice a day.

Mode of Administration : Take in the morning & evening on empty stomach with milk / luke–warm water / decoction of *Arjuna*–bark (to be prepared as mentioned below i.e. in group 'C').

(C) *DIVYA* ARJUNA KVĀTHA – 300 gms.

Dose : 1 teaspoon.

Mode of Administration : Boil one teaspoon of powder with one cup of cow's milk + 3 cups of water till it is reduced to one cup, and then strain it out. Take medicine of group 'B' with this decoction.

Prohibitions : Avoid ghee, oil, fried food, heavy & fast food & preparations of fine flour (*maida*). Bowels should be clear i.e. there should no constipation.

Note : Practice of *prāṇāyāmas* (breathing exercise), prescribed by honourable Swāmī Rāma Deva Ji is very necessary. It should be done regularly & slowly.

(18) MIGRAINE, CHRONIC HEADACHE & DEPRESSION

(A) *DIVYA* MEDHĀ KVĀTHA – 300 gms.

Dose : 1 teaspoon (5 gms.), twice a day.

Mode of Administration : Soak 1 teaspoon of this powder in 400 ml. of water at night, preferably in an earthen pot. In the morning, boil it till it remains 100ml. strain it out & take on empty stomach. For night dose, soak in the morning & boil in the same manner, & take before sleep.

(B) 1. ***DIVYA* MOTĪ PIṢṬĪ** — **4 gms.**
2. ***DIVYA* PRAVĀLA PIṢṬĪ** — **10 gms.**
3. ***DIVYA* GODANTĪ BHASMA** — **10 gms.**

Mode of Administration : Mix all these medicines together, divide into 60 parts, make packets, take each an hour before breakfast & dinner with honey.

Note : If disease is very chronic, then 1 – 2 gms. of *Rasarāja Rasa* should be added to group B which will be exceedingly beneficial.

(C) *DIVYA* MEDHĀ VAṬĪ :

Dose : 2 – 2 tabs., twice a day.

Mode of Administration : Take after breakfast & dinner with luke-warm water/milk.

(19) JOINT PAIN, GOUT, KNEE-JOINT PAIN, ETC.

(A) 1. ***DIVYA* SVARṆA-MĀKṢIKA BHASMA** — **5 gms.**
2. ***DIVYA* MAHĀ VĀTA VIDHVAṂSANA RASA** — **10 gms.**
3. ***DIVYA* PRAVĀLA PIṢṬĪ** — **10 gms.**
4. ***DIVYA* BṚHAD VĀTA CINTĀMAṆI RASA** — **1 gm.**

Mode of Administration : Mix all these medicines, divide into 60 parts, make packets, take each an hour before breakfast & dinner with honey or hot water.

Note : If there is severe pain, then the quantity of ***'Bṛhad Vāta Cintāmaṇi'*** may be increased to 2–3 gms. In newly occurring & less pain, above medicine excluding last one (i.e. *Bṛhad Vāta Cintāmaṇi*) is also very useful.

(B)	1. *DIVYA* YOGA RĀJA GUGGULU	60 gms.	**Dose :** 1 – 1 tab. from each. **Mode of Administration :** To be taken after breakfast, lunch & dinner with hot water / milk.
	2. *DIVYA* CANDRAPRABHĀ VAṬĪ	60 gms.	
	3. *DIVYA* PUNARNAVĀDI MAṆḌŪRA	40 gms.	

(20) SCIATICA & CERVICAL SPONDYLITIS

(A)	1. *DIVYA* EKĀṄGAVĪRA RASA	10 gms.	**Mode of Administration :** Mix all these four medicines together, divide into 60 parts, make packets, take each twice on empty stomach in the morning & evening with honey, warm water / milk.
	2. *DIVYA* PRAVĀLA PIṢṬĪ	10 gms.	
	3. *DIVYA* BṚHAD VĀTA CINTĀMAṆI RASA	1 gm.	
	4. *DIVYA* SVARṆA-MĀKṢIKA BHASMA	5 gms.	

(B)	1. *DIVYA* TRAYODAŚĀṄGA GUGGULU	60 gms.	**Dose :** 1–1 tab. from each. **Mode of Administration :** Take thrice a day after breakfast, lunch & dinner with hot water/milk..
	2. *DIVYA* CANDRA-PRABHĀ VAṬĪ	60 gms.	
	3. *DIVYA* PĪḌĀNTAKA RASA	40 gms.	

Prohibitions : Avoid curd (yoghurt), butter-milk, sour things, *māṣa (urad dal)*, cauli–flower.

(21) SINUSITIS, ASTHMA, CHRONIC RHINITIS & CORYZA

(A)
1. *DIVYA* ŚVĀSĀRI RASA 20 gms.
2. *DIVYA* ŚṚṄGA BHASMA 10 gms.
3. *DIVYA* ABHRAKA BHASMA 5 gms.
4. *DIVYA* PRAVĀLA PIṢṬĪ 5 gms.
5. *DIVYA* TRIKAṬU CŪRṆA 25 gms.

Mode of Administration : Mix all these medicines together, divide into 60 parts, take each an hour before breakfast & dinner with honey or warm water.

Note : For chronic patients, 2–3 gms. of ***Svarṇa B(V)asantamālatī*** should be added to the above medicines.

(B)
1. *DIVYA* LAKṢMĪ VILĀSA RASA 40 gms.
2. *DIVYA* SAÑJĪVANĪ VAṬĪ 40 gms.

Dose : 1 tab. from each twice / thrice a day.

Mode of Administration : Take after meals i.e. after breakfast, lunch & dinner with hot milk / water.

Prohibitions : Avoid ghee, oil, sour things, banana, ice-cream & other cold things. Always take hot water.

(22) PSORIASIS & ECZEMA

(A) *DIVYA* KĀYĀ-KALPA KVĀTHA :

Mode of Administration : Boil one teaspoon (5gm) of this medicine by adding 400ml of water till it reduces to 100 ml., strain it out, & take twice on empty stomach, before breakfast & dinner.

(B)
1. *DIVYA* RASA MĀṆIKYA 1 gm.
2. *DIVYA* PRAVĀLA PIṢṬĪ 10 gms.
3. *DIVYA* KĀYĀ-KALPA VAṬĪ 20 gms.
4. *DIVYA* AMṚTĀ SAT 10 gms.
5. *DIVYA* TĀLA SINDŪRA 1 gm.

Mode of Administration : Mix all these five medicines together, divide into 60 parts, take each part twice on empty stomach – an hour before breakfast & dinner with honey / hot water.

(C)*DIVYA* KAIŚORA GUGGULU – 60 gms.

Dose : 2–2 tabs., twice a day.

Mode of Administration : Take after breakfast & dinner with water.

(D)*DIVYA* ĀROGYA VARDHANĪ – 20 gms.

Dose : 1–1 tab., twice a day.

Mode of Administration : Take after breakfast & dinner with water.

(E) MAHĀ MAÑJIṢṬHĀRIṢṬA :

Dose : 4 teaspoonfuls twice daily.

Mode of Administration : Take after food by adding 4 teaspoonfuls of water.

(F) *DIVYA* KĀYĀ-KALPA TAILA :

Mode of Administration : Apply externally on affected part, twice daily.

Note : If the patient suffers from diarrhoea due to the intake of group A, then its dose should be reduced.

(23) CANCER (KARKAṬĀRBUDA)

(A) 1. *DIVYA* KĀYĀ-KALPA KVĀTHA	**100 gms.**	**Mode of Administration :** Mix both of these medicines together, boil one teaspoon (5 gms.) with 400 ml. of water till 100 ml. remains, strain it out, & take before breakfast & dinner.
2. *DIVYA* SARVA-KALPA KVĀTHA	**100 gms.**	

(B)	1. *DIVYA* SAÑJĪVANĪ VAṬĪ	10 gms.	**Mode of Administration :** Mix all these nine medicines, divide into 90 parts, take each part one hour before breakfast, lunch & dinner with honey / hot water.
	2. *DIVYA* ŚILĀ SINDŪRA	3 gms.	
	3. *DIVYA* TĀMRA BHASMA	1 gm.	
	4. *DIVYA* AMṚTĀ SATTVA	10 gms.	
	5. *DIVYA* ABHRAKA BHASMA	5 gms.	
	6. *DIVYA* HĪRAKA BHASMA	300–500 mgs.	
	7. *DIVYA* SVARṆA BASANTA MĀLATĪ	2–4 gms.	
	8. *DIVYA* MUKTĀ PIṢṬĪ	4 gms.	
	9. *DIVYA* PRAVĀLA PAÑCĀMṚTA	5 gms.	

Note : If the patient is suffering from lungs-cancer, then *ABHRAKA BHASMA* = 5gms., should be added to group 'B'.

(C)	1. *DIVYA* KAÑCANĀRA GUGGULU	60 gms.	**Dose :** 2–2 tabs from each, twice a daily. **Mode of Administration :** Take after breakfast or lunch & dinner with hot water/ milk. **Note** : If patient is unable to swallow the tablet, then it should be made to a powder & dose should be reduced.
	2. *DIVYA* VṚDDHIVĀDHIKĀ VAṬĪ	40 gms.	

(D)	1. Cow's urine	25 ml.
	2. Fresh Juice of *Guḍūcī* (*Tinospora cordifolia*)	25 ml.
	3. Leaves of *Tulasī* (Holy Basil)	5 – 7 (in number)
	4. Neem Leaves	3 – 4 (in number)

Note :

(i) The patient of cancer should take the medicines of group 'D' also in addition in the above, twice a day in the morning & evening (preferably on empty stomach).

(ii) In the case of cancer, dose may be reduced or increased according to the nature (constitution) of the patient & the seriousness of the disease. If patient is taking Chemo or Radiation therapy, even then this medicine reduces the adverse effects of the therapies, & controls the development of the disease.

(24) FIBROID UTERUS *(GARBHĀŚAYĀRBUDA)*

(A)	**1. *DIVYA* ŚILĀ SINDŪRA**	**3 gms.**	**Mode of Administration :** Mix all these medicines together, divide into 60 parts, take each an hour before breakfast & dinner with honey or warm water.
	2. *DIVYA* VṚDDHIVĀDHIKĀ	**10 gms.**	
	3. *DIVYA* KAHARAVĀ PIṢṬĪ	**10 gms.**	
	4. *DIVYA* MUKTĀ PIṢṬĪ	**3 gms.**	
	5. *DIVYA* AMṚTĀ SATTVA	**10 gms.**	
	6. *DIVYA* SPHAṬIKA BHASMA	**5 gms.**	

(B)	**1. *DIVYA* KĀÑCANĀRA GUGGULU**	**60 gms.**	**Dose :** 1-1 tab. from each, thrice a daily. **Mode of Administration :** Take after breakfast, lunch & dinner with water.
	2. *DIVYA* STRĪ RASĀYANA VAṬĪ	**60 gms.**	

(25) MENORRHAGIA (HEAVY MENSTRUATION) & AMENORRHOEA(LESS MENSTRUATION)

(A)
1. *DIVYA* PRAVĀLA PIṢṬĪ 10 gms.
2. *DIVYA* KAHARAVĀ PIṢṬĪ 10 gms.
3. *DIVYA* AMṚTĀ SATTVA 10 gms.
4. *DIVYA* MUKTĀ PIṢṬĪ 4 gms.
5. *DIVYA* VASANTAKUSUMĀ-KARA RASA 1 gm.

Mode of Administration : Mix all these five medicines together, divide into 60 parts, take each an hour before breakfast & dinner with honey or warm water.

(B) *DIVYA* STRĪ RASĀYANA VAṬĪ – 60 gms.

Dose : 2 tabs., twice a day.

Mode of Administration : Take after breakfast (or lunch) & dinner with milk / water.

Note : Use of the leaves of *śiṃśapā* or *śīśama* (*Dalbergia sissoo*) is exceedingly useful in menorrhagia (excessive bleeding).

(26) HEPATITIS A, B & C (*YAKṚT–ŚOTHA*)

(A) *DIVYA* SARVA–KALPA KVĀTHA – 300 gms.

Mode of Administration : Boil one teaspoon (5 gms.) of this medicine with 400 ml. of water till it reduces to 100 ml., strain it out, & take before breakfast & dinner. [For details : vide. : Ch. 1, P. no. 18.]

(B)
1. *DIVYA* PRAVĀLA PAÑCĀMṚTA 10 gms.
2. *DIVYA* KĀSĪSA BHASMA 5 gms.
3. *DIVYA* SVARṆA-MĀKṢIKA BHASMA 5 gms.
4. *DIVYA* AMṚTĀ SATTVA 10 gms.
5. *DIVYA* SVARṆA B(V)ASANTA MĀLATĪ 3 gms.

Mode of Administration : Mix all these medicines together, divide into sixty parts, take one part on hour before breakfast & dinner with honey or warm water.

(C)	1. *DIVYA* UDARĀMṚTA VAṬĪ	60 gms.	**Dose :** One tab. from each, twice a day. **Mode of Administration :** Take after breakfast / dinner with luke-warm water / milk.
	2. *DIVYA* ĀROGYAVARDHANĪ VAṬĪ	40 gms.	
	3. *DIVYA* PUNAR-NAVĀDI MAṆḌŪRA	40 gms.	

(D) ŚYONĀKA KVĀTHA – 300 gms.

Mode of Administration : Soak 10 gms. (2 teaspoons) of medicine in 300 gms. of water in an earthen vessel at night, crush it well in the morning, strain it out & take on empty stomach.

Prohibitions : Avoid oily things, fried food, sour things, citrus fruits, hot & strong spices, alcohol, tea, coffee & cold drinks.

(27) CIRRHOSIS OF LIVER

(A)	1. *DIVYA* SARVA-KALPA KVĀTHA	200 gms.	**Mode of Administration :** Boil one teaspoon (5 gms.) of this medicine by adding 400 ml. of water till it reduces to 100 ml., take twice on empty stomach, before breakfast & dinner.
	2. *DIVYA* KĀYĀ-KALPA KVĀTHA	100 gms.	

(B)	1. *DIVYA* PRAVĀLA PAÑCĀMṚTA	10 gms.	**Mode of Administration :** Mix all these five medicines together, divide into 60 parts, take each part two or three times per day, before breakfast, lunch & dinner with honey or water.
	2. *DIVYA* SVARṆA-MĀKṢIKA BHASMA	5 gms.	
	3. *DIVYA* KĀSĪSA BHASMA	5 gms.	
	4. *DIVYA* SVARṆA BASANTA MĀLATĪ	2 gms.	
	5. *DIVYA* AMṚTĀ SAT	10 gms.	

(C) 1. *DIVYA* UDARĀMṚTA VAṬĪ	60 gms.	**Dose :** 1-1 tab., from each, two / three times per day. **Mode of Administration :** Take after breakfast, lunch & dinner with luke-warm water.
2. *DIVYA* ĀROGYA-VARDHANĪ VAṬĪ	40 gms.	

(28) CHRONIC RENAL FAILURE

(A) ***DIVYA VṚKKA DOṢA-HARA KVĀTHA*** **- 200 gms.**

Mode of Administration: Boil one teaspoonful (5 gms.) of the mixture of both these medicines + bark of *pīpala* or *Ficus religios* (5 gms.) + bark of *nimba* or *Azadirachta indica* (5 gms.) by adding 400 ml. of water till 100 ml. remains, strain it out, and take before breakfast & dinner.

(B) 1. *DIVYA* AMṚTĀ SATTVA	10 gms.	**Mode of Administration :** Mix all these four medicines together, divide into 60 parts, take each dose one hour before breakfast & dinner with honey or warm water.
2. *DIVYA* BASANTA KUSUMĀKARA RASA	1 gm.	
3. *DIVYA* HAJARULA YAHŪDA BHASMA	10 gms.	
4. *DIVYA* PUNARNAVĀDI MAṆḌŪRA	10 gms.	

Note : If patient is suffering from diabetes, then group 'B' should be taken either with group 'A' or water.

(C) 1. *DIVYA* CANDRA-PRABHĀ VAṬĪ	40 gms.	**Dose :** 1 tab. from both twice a day. **Mode of Administration:** Take after breakfast & dinner with water.
2. *DIVYA* GOKṢURĀDI GUGGULU	40 gms.	

Note : If patient is suffering from high blood pressure, then he should take 1-2 tabs. of "***MUKTĀ VAṬĪ***" twice on empty stomach with fresh water or decoction group 'A'

(29) HERNIA *(ĀNTRA-VṚDDHI)*

(A) 1. ***DIVYA TRIKAṬU CŪRṆA***	**25 gms.**	**Mode of Administration :** Mix all these medicines together, divide into 60 parts, take each of them twice on empty stomach, one hour before breakfast & dinner with honey / hot water.
2. ***DIVYA PRAVĀLA PIṢṬĪ***	**10 gms.**	
3. ***DIVYA GODANTĪ BHASMA***	**10 gms**	

(B) ***DIVYA SARVA-KALPA KVĀTHA*- 300 gms.**

Mode of Administration : Boil one teaspoonful (5 gms.) of this medicine with 400 ml. of water till 100 ml. remains, strain it out & take twice on empty stomach in the morning & evening.

(C) 1. ***DIVYA VṚDDHIVĀDHIKĀ VAṬĪ***	**40 gms.**	**Dose :** 2-2 tabs. from each, twice a day. **Mode of Administration :** Take twice after lunch or breakfast & dinner with hot water.
2. ***DIVYA KĀÑCANĀRA GUGGULU***	**60 gms.**	

(30) EPILEPSY *(APASMĀRA)*

(A) ***DIVYA MEDHĀ KVĀTHA* – 300 gms.**

Mode of Administration: Boil one teaspoon (5 gms.) of this medicine with 40 ml of water till it is reduced to 10 ml. & take twice on empty stomach before breakfast & dinner.

(B) 1. ***DIVYA MUKTĀ PIṢṬĪ***	**4 gms.**	**Mode of Administration :** Mix all these medicines together, divide into 60 parts, take each of them an hour before breakfast and dinner with honey/ hot water.
2. ***DIVYA PRAVĀLA PIṢṬĪ***	**10 gms.**	
3. ***DIVYA AMṚTĀ SATTVA***	**10 gms.**	
4. ***DIVYA* KAPARDAKA *BHASMA***	**10 gms.**	

Note : If disease is chronic then 1-2 gms. of ***RASARĀJA RASA*** should be added to group 'B' which will be exceedingly beneficial.

(C) ***DIVYA MEDHĀ VAṬĪ*** **- 60 gms.**

Dose : 2-2 tabs., twice a day.

Mode of Administration : Take after lunch (or breakfast) & dinner with hot water/milk.

(D) ***SĀRASVATĀRIṢṬA***

Dose : 4 teaspoonfull twice a day.

Mode of Administration : Take after lunch & dinner by adding four teaspoons of water.

(31) CATARACT & GLAUCOMA

(A)

1. ***DIVYA ĀMALAKĪ RASĀYANA***	**200 gms.**	**Dose :** 1 teaspoon, twice daily. **Mode of Administration :** Mix all these three medicines well, take before breakfast & dinner with fresh water/honey.
2. ***DIVYA SAPTĀMṚTA LAUHA***	**20 gms.**	
3. ***DIVYA MUKTĀ ŚUKTI BHASMA***	**10 gms.**	

(B) ***DIVYA MAHĀ TRIPHALĀ GHṚTA*** **- 200 ml.**

Dose : 1 teaspoon, twice a day.

Mode of Administration : Take on empty stomach in the morning & evening with milk.

(C) ***DIVYA NETRA JYOTI*** **:** For external use only.

Mode of Administration : Apply one drop in each eye twice in the morning & evening.

(32) INFERTILITY (*BANDHYATVA*)

(A)

1. ***DIVYA ŚIVALIṄGĪ BĪJA***	**100 gms.**	**Dose :** 1 gm. twice a day. **Mode of Administration :** Make a fine powder of both these drugs, take an hour before breakfast & dinner with milk of cow having calf.
2. ***DIVYA PUTRAJĪVAKA GIRĪ***	**100 gms.**	

(B) ***PHALA GHṚTA***

Dose : 1 teaspoon, twice a day.

Mode of Administration : Take on empty stomach in the morning & evening with cow's milk.

(C) 1. *DIVYA STRĪ RASĀYANA VAṬĪ*	60 gms.	**Dose :** 2-2 tabs. from both, twice a day. **Mode of Administration :** Take after breakfast & dinner with luke-warm water.
2. *DIVYA CANDRA-PRABHĀ VAṬĪ*	60 gms.	

Note : If patient is suffering from amenorrhoea (less bleeding during menstruation) then following medicines should be taken additionally:

(D) *RAJAḤ PRAVARTANĪ VAṬĪ*

Dose : 2-2 tabs. twice a day.

Mode of Administration : Take on empty stomach in the morning & evening with milk.

(E) *DIVYA DAŚAMŪLA KVĀTHA*

Mode of Administration : Boil one teaspoon (5 gms.) with 400 ml. of water till 100 ml. remains, strain it out & take after breakfast & dinner.

(33) CONSTIPATION

(A) *DIVYA ABHAYĀRIṢṬA*

Dose : 3 teaspoon, twice a day.

Mode of Administration : Take after lunch or breakfast & dinner by adding three teaspoons of luke-warm water.

(B) *DIVYA UDARA-KALPA CŪRṆA* **OR** *DIVYA CŪRṆA*

Dose : 1 teaspoon.

Mode of Administration : Take at bed time with hot water.

Note : Patient, suffering from diabetes should not take ***"Divya Udara-kalpa Cūrṇa"***.

(34) PARKINSONISM (*KAMPA-VĀTA*)

(A) 1. *DIVYA EKĀṄGAVĪRA RASA*	10 gms.	**Mode of Administration :** mix all these medicines together, divede in to 60 doses, take each of them twice/ thrice daily before break fast, lunch & dinner with honey or water.
2. *DIVYA SVARṆ-AMĀKṢIKA BHASMA*	5 gms.	
3. DIVYA PRAVĀLA *PIṢṬĪ*	10 gms.	
4. *DIVYA RASARĀJA RASA*	1 gm.	
5. *DIVYA AMṚTĀ SAT*	10 gms.	
6. *DIVYA MAKARADHVAJA*	2 gms.	

(B) 1. *DIVYA TRAYODAŚĀṄGA GUGGULU*	60 gms.	**Dose :** 2-2 tabs. from each, thrice daily. **Mode of Administration :** Take after breakfast, lunch & dinner with luke-warm water.
2. *DIVYA* CANDRA-PRABHĀVAṬĪ	60 gms.	
3. *DIVYA* MEDHĀ VAṬĪ	60 gms.	

(C) ***DIVYA*** **ŚILĀJĪTA SAT - 20 gms.**

Dose : 1-2 drops, twice daily.

Mode of Administration : Take in the morning & evening with milk.

(35) OSTEOPOROSIS *(ASTHI-SUṢIRATĀ)*

(A) 1. *DIVYA AMṚTĀ SAT*	10 gms.	**Mode of Administration :** Mix all these medicines together, divide into 60 doses, take each of them twice or thrice daily, before breakfast, lunch & dinner with honey or water.
2. *DIVYA SVARṆA-MĀKṢIKA*	5 gms.	
3. *DIVYA* PRAVĀLA PIṢṬĪ	10 gms.	
4. *DIVYA GODANTĪ BHASMA*	5 gms.	
5. *DIVYA BṚHAD VĀTA CINTĀMAṆI*	1 gm.	

(B)	1. *DIVYA YOGA RĀJA GUGGULU*	60 gms.	**Dose :** 2-2 tabs. each of these three medicines, twice daily. **Mode of Administration :** Take after breakfast & dinner with luke-warm water.
	2. *DIVYA* CANDRA-PRABHĀ VAṬĪ	60 gms.	
	3. *DIVYA ŚILĀJĪTA RASĀYANA*	40 gms.	

(C) *DIVYA AŚVAGANDHĀRIṢṬA*

Dose : 4 teaspoons, twice a day.

Mode of Administration : Take after breakfast (or lunch) & dinner by adding 4 teaspoons of luke-warm water followed by group B.

(36) OTORRHAGIA, TYMPANITIS & DEAFNESS

(A)	1. *DIVYA SĀRIVĀDI VAṬĪ*	**Dose :** 1-1 tab. from each, twice a day. **Mode of Administration :** Take in the morning & evening with milk / water.
	2. *DIVYA CANDRA-PRABHĀ VAṬĪ*	
	3. *DIVYA ŚILĀJĪTA RASĀYANA*	

(B) *DIVYA KĀYĀ-KALPA TAILA*

Mode of Administration : Pour 2-2 drops in each ear, twice a day.

CHAPTER - IV
MIRACULOUS HOME REMEDIES FOR DIFFERENT DISEASES PRESCRIBED BY SWAMI RAM DEVJI IN *YOGA*–CAMPS

(1) GRUEL : CURE FOR OBESITY & DIABETES

1. **Wheat**	-	**500 gms.**	3. **Millet**	-	**500 gms.**
2. **Rice**	-	**500 gms.**	4. **Moong dal**	-	**500 gms.**

Method of Preparation : All these corns should be mixed together, roasted on mild fire & ground coarsely. To this, 20gms. of *ajavāyana* & 50 gms. of white til (sesame seeds) should be added. 50 gms. (or according to requirement) of this mixture should be cooked with 400ml. of water by adding vegetables (according to taste) & little salt. This should be taken regularly for 15 to 30 days, which cures diabetes. It definitely reduces the weight of a heart patient who is suffering from obesity too.

(2) EYE-DROPS-NETRA-JYOTI : CURE FOR CATARACT & GLAUCOMA

1. **Juice of White Onion** **10 ml.**
2. **Ginger Juice** **10 ml.**
3. **Lemon Juice** **10 ml.**
4. **Honey** **50 ml.**

Method of Preparation : Mix all these drugs together.

Mode of Administration : Apply two drops in each eye regularly.

Therapeutic Uses : Cures cataract and glaucoma by gradually reducing the pressure (tension) of the eye.

Note : This medicine is specially prepared in Ashram in the name of *'Divya Netra-jyoti'*. Many patients have got relief by the use of this medicine.

(3) TOOTH-POWDER : CURE FOR ALL TYPES OF TOOTH-DISEASES

1. ***Haridrā*** **(Turmeric)** **100 gms.**
2. ***Sphaṭika*** **(Alum)** **100 gms.**

3. **Bark of *Babbūla*** **100 gms.**
4. ***Tumburu* (Seed)** **50 gms.**
5. ***Bibhītaka*** **50 gms.**
6. **Rock-salt** **100 gms.**
7. **Neem - leaf** **100 gms.**
8. ***Akarakarā* (flower)** **50 gms.**
9. ***Lavaṅga* or clove (outer covering)** **20 gms.**

Method of Preparation : All these drugs should be taken in mentioned quantities and made to a very fine powder.

Therapeutic Uses : Cures *danta-kṛmi* (bacterial infection in tooth), pyorrhoea, etc. by root.

Note : In ashram, this tooth-powder is prepared by adding some other drugs (herbs) also, and is named as '*Divya Danta-mañjana*'.

(4) JUICE OF SWEET GOURD : USEFUL FOR HEART-DISEASES, HYPER ACIDITY, ABDOMINAL DISEASES & OBESITY

1. **Gourd** **500 gms.**
2. **Mint leaves** **7 leaves**
3. ***Tulasī* (Holy Basil) leaves** **7 leaves**

Method of Preparation : All the above mentioned ingredients should be made to a paste and juice should be squeezed out.

Mode of Administration : Take one cup on empty stomach in the morning.

Therapeutic Uses : Cures the coronary blockage, hyper acidity & different types of abdominal diseases.

Note : It should be taken regularly.

(5) BARK OF ARJUNA : KṢĪRA PĀKA (Milk Preparation)

1. **Powder of *Arjuna* bark** (bark of *Terminalia arjuna*) **5-10 gms.**
2. **Milk** **1 cup**
3. **Water** **3 cups**

Method of Preparation : All these ingredients should be boiled together till it is reduced to one cup & strained it out.

Mode of Administration : Take in the morning on empty stomach.

Therapeutic Uses : Regular intake is very useful for weakness of heart.

(6) INFALLIBLE REMEDY FOR JAUNDICE, HEPATITIS & CIRRHOSIS OF LIVER

1.	**Bark of *Śyonaka***	**25 gms.**
2.	***Bhūmyāmalakī* (whole plant)**	**25 gms.**
3.	***Punarnavā* (root)**	**25 gms.**

Method of Preparation : All the above mentioned fresh drugs should be taken in prescribed quantity, made to a paste, and the juice should be squeezed out.

Mode of Administration : To be taken in the morning regularly on empty stomach.

Therapeutic Uses : Definitey cures jaundice & hepatitis.

Note :

1. If these drugs are not available, then '*Sarva Kalpa Kvātha*' , prepared in the Ashram can be used. It is also prepared with dry root of *punarnavā* (*Boerhavia diffusa*), *bhūmyāmalakī* or *bhūmi-amala* (*Phyllanthus niruri*) & *śyonāka* (*Oroxylum indicum*) among others.
2. For detailed information about the cure of jaundice, hepatitis etc. vide Ch. III, no. 26-Hepatitis A,B,C. p. 41

(7) INFALLIBLE HOME REMEDY FOR CHRONIC COUGH

Black Pepper 5-7 (in number) **for whole day**

Mode of Administration : 2-3 black peppers should be kept (at a time) in the mouth & chewed slowly. Thus, 5-7 peppers should lbe chewed in the whole day.

Therapeutic Uses : It gives instant relief in chronic cough. We have experience of the cure of many years old (chronic) cough within few minutes only.

(8) INFALLIBLE HOME REMEDY FOR DRY & BLEEDING PILES

1. Camphor (native) - ½ gm.

2. Banana - 1 piece

Mode of Administration : Keep a piece of no. 1 (camphor) in a piece of banana, & should be swallowed on an empty stomach.

Therapeutic Uses : It stops bleeding with one dose only . If bleeding does not stop with one dose, then it should be repeated for three times, but not more than thrice.

(9) USE OF LEMON & MILK : FOR BLEEDING PILES

Mode of Administration : Take one cup of warm (drinkable warm) cow's milk, squeeze out the juice of ½ lemon into this and take it immediately before being reduced to cheese.

Therapeutic Uses : Immediately stops the bleeding of piles.

Precaution :

i. Don't repeat this remedy more than twice.

ii. If necessary consult the physician.

(10) LEAVES OF ŚĪŚAMA OR ŚIṂŚAPĀ (*DALBERGIA SISSOO*) - EXTREMELY USEFUL IN LEUCORRHOEA, *PRAMEHA* (OBSTINATE URINARY DISORDERS INCLUDING DIABETES); *DHĀTU-ROGA* (SEMINAL DISEASES) & MENORRHAGIA

1. Leaves of *śīśama* - 8-10 leaves
(*Dalbergia sissoo*)
2. *Miśrī* (Candied sugar) - 25 gms.

one dose

Mode of Administration : Both of these drugs should be made to a paste together, & taken in the morning.

Therapeutic Uses : Definitely cures leucorrhoea of women, *prameha* (obstinate urinary disorders including diabetes) in males, & menorrhagia (heavy menstruation) in females. It is also very useful and is harmless medicine for the cure of bleeding caused by heat; very cooling medicine intake which is convent.

Note :

i. In winter 4-5 seeds of black pepper should be added to it as it is exceedingly cold.

ii. Patients suffering from diabetes should take this without adding *miśrī* (candied sugar).

(11) HOME REMEDY FOR PILES & MENORRHAGIA

BROWN FIBERS OF COCONUT IN ASH FORM

Method of Preparation : Outer fibers of coconut should be burnt, made to ash & seived.

(A) Dose : 3 gms., thrice a day (only for one day).

Mode of Administration : Take on empty stomach (in the morning, after noon & evening) with butter-milk.

Therapeutic Uses : Cures piles, menorrhagia (in menstruation) & leucorrhoea.

(B) Dose : 1 gm., thrice a day.

Mode of Administration : To be taken with a little quantity of water.

Therapeutic Uses : Cures vomiting, cholera & hiccup.

(12) HOME REMEDY FOR HIC-CUP

Mayūra-piccha Bhasma **(ash of peacock-feather)**

Dose : ¼ gm., 2-3 times a day.

Mode of Administration : Take on empty stomach with honey.

Therapeutic Uses : Cures hiccup immediately.

(13) USE OF GALACTAGOGUE : FOR MOTHERS

Śatāvara Cūrṇa **(Powder of *Asparagus racemosus*)**

Dose : 3-5 gms., twice daily.

Mode of Administration : To be taken on empty stomach with cow's milk.

Therapeutic Uses : It promotes lactation if there is loss or less quantity of lactation in mothers.

Note :

1. During pregnancy, regular intake of 2-3 gms. of the powder of *śatāvara* (*Asparagus racemosus*) in general, is also useful. It maintains the proper quantity of lactation after delivery. Mothers should take this medicine regularly after delivery.

2. If 50 gms. of this powder, twice daily (in the morning & evening), is also given to cows & buffaloes it increases the quantity of milk in them irregularly.

(14) JUICE OF WHEAT-GRASS : CURE FOR CANCER & AIDS

Method of Preparation : Wheat should be sown in nine different flower-pots or in nine spots on a piece of small land. Sowing should be done in each pot or spot one by one for nine days continuously. On the tenth day, green leaves of grown wheat should be cut from the first flower pot. 10 gms. of these leaves and 25 gms. (equal to two feet long and one finger in thickness) of a stem of *guḍūcī* (*Tinospora cordifolia*) should be ground by adding some water. Out of this paste, juice is to be squeezed out through a piece of clean cloth. Then from the second day (i.e. eleventh day) onwards, same procedure should be followed by taking out leaves from the second pot, third pot, and so on.

Dose : One cup on empty stomach.

Note :

(i) In each empty flower pot, wheat should be sown again on the same day, and the same process should be repeated continuously on each succeeding day.

(ii) Intake of this juice along with the medicines given by the physician of Ashram helps a lot in curing the dangerous and serious diseases, like concer, AIDS, etc.

(15) BARK OF AŚVATTHA OR PĪPALA+NEEM+ SARVAKALPA KVĀTHA+VṚKKADOṢA-HARA KVĀTHA

1. Neem - bark powder	**5 gms.**	One dose
2. *Pīpala (Ficus reliogosa)*-bark powder	**5 gms.**	

Method of Preparation : 5 gms. powder of each of these both drugs should be boiled with 400 gms. of water till it is reduced to 100 gms. & then strained out.

Mode of Administration : To be taken twice on empty stomach an hour before breakfast & dinner.

Therapeutic Uses : It reduces the excessive quantity of Urea & Creatinine in blood.

(16) HOME REMEDY FOR THYROID , TONSILITIS & KAPHA-ROGAS

1. Powder of *Trikaṭu*	**50 gms.**
2. Powder of *Bidhītaka* (*Terminalia belerica*)	**20 gms.**
3. *Pravāla piṣṭi*	**10 gms.**

Method of Preparation : Powder of all the above three drugs should be mixed together.

Dose :

For adult : 1-1 gm., twice a day.

For child : ½ - ½ gm., twice a day.

Method of Administration : To be taken twice on empty stomach (in the morning & evening) with honey.

Therapeutic Uses : Cures thyroid problems & tonsilitis of children; also useful in asthma & diseases caused by the aggravation of *kapha* (*kapha-rogas*).

(17) HOME REMEDY FOR KAPHA-DISEASES (DISEASES CAUSED BY AGGRAVATED KAPHA)

1. Almond pulp	**100 gms.**
2. Brown sugar	**50 gms.**
3. *Marica* (Black pepper)	**20 gms.**

Method of Preparation : All the above three drugs should be made to a powder & mixed together.

Dose : One teaspoon.

Mode of Administration : To be taken after dinner with luke-warm milk.

Therapeutic Uses : Cures chronic *kapha*-diseases (diseases caused by aggravated *kapha*), chronic rhinitis, coryza & sinusitis; also removes constipation.

Note :

i) Patients suffering from diabetes should not add brown sugar i.e. no. 2.

ii) Patients suffering from hyper acidity (*amla-pitta*) should add only 10 gms. of Black pepper (no.3).

(18) HOME REMEDIES FOR VĀTA-ROGAS (DISEASES CAUSED BY THE AGGRAVAATION OF VĀTA OR VĀYU)

(A) Powder of *Withania Somnifera*

1.	***Haridrā* (Turmeric)**	**100 gms.**
2.	***Methī dānā* (Fenugreek seeds)**	**100 gms.**
3.	***Śuṇthī* (Dry ginger)**	**100 gms.**
4.	***Aśvagandhā cūrṇa***	**50 gms.**

Method of Preparation : All these four drugs should be made to a powder & mixed together.

Dose : One teaspoon, twice a day

Mode of Administration : Take after breakfast & dinner with luke-warm water.

(B) *Laśuna* or *Garlic*

Dose : 1-3 cloves.

Mode of Administration : On empty stomach in the morning, with water.

Therapeutic Uses : Reduces the increased quantity of cholesterol & Triglyceride, also removes the blockage of coronary arteries (coronary thrombosis).

(C) Rhizome of *Musta (Cyperus rotundus)*

Method of Preparation : Take rhizome of *musta* & made to a powder.

Dose : 1-2 gm., twice daily.

Mode of Administration : To be taken in the morning & evening with water / milk.

Therapeutic Uses : Marvellous remedy for the cure of joint pains & rheumatoid arthritis.

(D) Leaves of *Nirguṇḍī (Vitex negundo)*

Method of Preparation : Leaves of this drug should be made to a powder.

Mode of Administration : To be taken after lunch & dinner with water.

Dose : one teaspoon, twice a day.

Therapeutic Uses : Cures *vātika* diseases (diseases caused by the aggravation of *vāta*).

(19) RECIPE FOR INFERTILITY

1. *Śivaliṅgī* bīja (Seeds of *Bryoina laciniosa*)	**100 gms.**
2. Pulp of *Putrajīvaka* (*Putranjiva roxburghii*)	**200 gms.**

Method of Preparation : Mix both of these drugs together & made to powder.

Dose : ¼th teaspoon, twice a day.

Mode of Administration : Take before breakfast & dinner with cow's milk.

Therapeutic Uses : Promotes fertility & brings about offspring immediately, also cures miscarriage.

(20) USE OF APĀMĀRGA FOR NORMAL DELIVERY

(A) Root of Apāmārga (*Achyranthes aspera*)

Mode of Administration : This root should be made into a ring shape. When labour pains start this ring should be tied on the navel (umblicus) of the coming mother. By this, mother delivers the child normally within 5-10 minutes. Even if there is no delivery, then the paste made by the powder of same root may also be applied around the naval over abdomen. Alternatively, this powder should be tied in a piece of cloth, made to bolus & kept inside the vagina which also results in a normal delivery.

Precaution : Ring made of the root of *Achyranthes aspera* (*apāmārga*), or paste of this powder, or bolus should be removed immediately after the delivery. Otherwise it will harm badly the body of the mother.

OTHER USAGE OF THE ROOT OF *APĀMĀRGA* (*Achyranthes aspera*)

(B) Root of *Apāmārga* (*Achyranthes aspera*)

Mode of Administration : To be used as tooth-brush.

Therapeutic Uses : It makes the teeth strong and cures tooth diseases including pyorrhoea (periodontal disease).

(C) Leaves of *Apāmārga* (*Achyranthes aspera*)

Mode of Administration : These leaves should be ground, made to a paste & applied over the place affected by cancer.

Therapeutic Uses : Useful in cancer.

(D) Seed of *Apāmārga* (*Achyranthes aspera*)

Mode of Administration : These seeds should be cooked like rice by adding milk and made to *kheer* (*pāyasa* - milk and rice preparation). This should be taken internally as food.

Therapeutic Uses : Cures *bhasmaka* (a condition in which digestive power of a person is excessively excited, which causes voracious hunger, and very heavy meal even taken in large quantity, gets digested in a very short period).

People suffering from voracious hunger control their hunger by the intake of this *kheer*. Many yogis also take this *kheer* of *apāmāgra* (*Achyranthes aspera*) before observing long fasting, so that hunger may not create problem for them.

(21) LEAF OF AŚVAGANDHĀ (WITHANIA SOMNIFERA) : EXCEEDINGLY USEFUL FOR OBESITY, DIABETES MELLITUS & HEART - DISEASES

Leaf of *Aśvagandhā* (*withania somnifera*)

Dose: One leaf, thrice a day.

Mode of Administration: One leaf should be washed, crushed with hand, made to a bolus, and taken on empty stomach an hour before breakfast, lunch & dinner with water for one week continuously.

Diet : Fruits, vegetables, milk, fruit-juice and butter-milk should be taken as food.

Therapeutic Uses : Reduces many kgs. of weight within a week.

Note : By the use of this simple remedy mentioned by honorable (Swami RamdevJi), lakhs of people have reduced their weight & become healthy.

(22) HOME REMEDIES FOR MADHUMEHA (DIABETES MELLITUS)

(A)

1. Cucumber	**1 in number**
2. Bitter gourd	**1 in number**
3. Tomato	**1 in number**

Mode of Administration : Juice should be squeezed out of the above-mentioned ingredients and taken internally on empty stomach in the morning.

(B) Stone of Jamun or Black-berry (*Syzygium cumini*)

Dose : Teaspoon, twice a day.

Mode of Administration : These seeds should be made to a paste & taken on empty stomach (in the morning & evening) with water.

(C) Neem (*Azadirachta indica*) Leaf

Dose : 7 leaves.

Mode of Administration : To be chewed as whole or made to a paste and taken with water.

(D) Flower of *Sadābahāra* (*Lochnera rosea*)

Dose : 7 flowers.

Mode of Administration : To be chewed followed by water, on empty stomach.

(E)

1. ***Giloy* or *Guḍūcī* (*Tinospora cordifolia*)**
2. **Jamun or black-berry (*Syzygium cumini*)**
3. ***Kuṭakī* (*Picrorhiza kurroa*)**
4. **Leaf of Neem (*Aazadirachta indica*)**
5. ***Kirāta tikta* or *Cirāyatā* (*Swertia chirata*)**
6. ***Kāla megha* or *Bhūnimba* (*Andrographis paniculata*)**
7. **Dry *Kāravellaka* or Bitter gourd (*Momordica charantia*)**
8. ***Kālī jīrī* or *Araṇya jīraka* (*Centratheum anthelmintion*)**
9. **Seeds of *Methī* or fenugreek (*Trigonella foenum-graecum*)**

Dose: One teaspoon, twice a day.

Mode of Administration : Take on empty stomach – in the morning & evening with water.

Method of Preparation : All these nine ingredients should be taken in equal quantity and made to a powder.

Therapeutic Uses : All the above five recipes are very useful for controlling diabetes.

(23) COW'S URINE : DIFFERENT USAGES

Contents : According to modern analysis, cow's urine contains nitrogen, phosphate, calcium, magnesium, urea, uric acid, potassium, sodium, carbolic acid , lactose and hormones. These contents release their effects in different ways to cure different diseases.

Dose : 10 – 15 ml., twice a day.

1. Mode of Administration: Fresh cow's urine should be sieved through eight-folded clean cloth piece and then taken internally. If fresh urine is not available then it may be stored in a clean bottle after sieving. Patients, who are not suffering from diabetes, should add honey to it. It will preserve the urine for a long period. Urine of a cow, who has freshly delivered a calf or who has to give a birth to calf after one or two months, should not be used.

Therapeutic Uses : Cures cancer, asthma, chronic renal failure, ascites and hepatitis A,B,C including other common diseases.

2. Mode of Administration : Cow's urine should be boiled in a copper vessel till it is reduced to its half. This should be strained and stored in a bottle. 1-2 drops of this urine should be poured into the eyes twice daily (in the morning & evening).

Therapeutic Uses : Useful in all types of eye-diseases.

(24) PĀṢĀṆABHEDA OR PATTHARACAṬṬĀ : FOR THE CURE OF STONE

Leaves of *Pattharacaṭṭā* (*Bergenia ligulata*)

Dose : 2 – 3 leaves.

Mode of Administration : Leaves of the above drug should be chewed daily in the morning.

Therapeutic Uses : Useful in all types of stone, urinary diseases & disorder related to gall bladder.

(25) LEAF OF PEEPAL OR FICUS RELIGIOSA FOR EPISTAXIS

(A) Leaf of Peepal (*Ficus religiosa*)

Dose : 5 – 5 drops in each nostril.

For Internal use : Juice of 30 – 40 leaves.

Mode of Administration : Leaves should be ground, made to a paste and juice should be squeezed out. This should be administered as follows : (1) to be dropped into both nostrils, and (2) to be taken internally by adding *miśrī* or candied sugar.

Therapeutic Uses : Cures epistaxis.

(B) For all Types of Bleeding

Dose : 5–10 ml.

Mode of Administration : To be taken in the morning on empty stomach.

(26) WATER OF SOAP-NUT (SAPINDUS TRIFOLIATUS) : USEFUL IN ASTHMA,COUGH, SINUSITIS, CHRONIC RHINITIS & HEADACHE

1. **Powder of Soap-nut (*Sapindus trifoliatus*)** **1 gm.**
2. **Powder of *Trikaṭu* (combination of dry ginger+ black pepper + long pepper)** **2-3 gms.**
3. **Water** **50 mg.**

Method of Preparation : Powders nos. 1+2 should be soaked in water (no.3) during night. In the morning, the water should be decanted and stored in a bottle.

Mode of Administration : 4-5 drops should be poured in each nostril in the morning on empty stomach.

Therapeutic Uses : It takes out the phlegm adhered inside, opens the blocked nostrils & relieves headache instantaneously.

(27) COSTLESS EXPERIENCE FOR STOPPAGE OF HAIR-FALL & GREYING OF HAIR

Mode of Administration : Nails of the fingers of both hands should be rubbed together for 5 minutes continuously twice or thrice a day regularly.

Therapeutic Uses : It stops the fall and graying of hair, makes the hair black & promotes their luxurious growth.

Note : We have good experience of growing of hairs on the thousand of hereditary bald heads , as well as the conversion of grey hair into black in the age of seventy years.

(28) INFALLIBLE HOME REMEDY FOR HAIR

1. **Bee-hive of Yellow bees from which bees have flown away** **25 gms.**
2. **Leaves of native variety of Shoe flower (*Hibiscus rosa-sinensis*)** **10-15 in numbers**
3. **Coconut oil** **500 ml.**

Method of Preparation : All the above mentioned ingredients should be cooked together on mild fire till bee-hive becomes black in colour. Then heating should be discontinued and oil should be allowed to cool. When it becomes cold, oil should be decanted and stored in a bottle.

Mode of Administration : To be massaged gently on the head daily.

Therapeutic Uses : It helps in growing hair.

(29) ANTI-DANDRUFF OIL (HOME REMEDY)

1.	**Juice of neem leaves**	**200 ml.**
2.	**Sesame oil**	**100 ml.**

Method of Preparation : Both of these drugs should be boiled together by applying mild fire till liquid gets burnt & only oil remains. Then it should be filtered and stored in a bottle.

Mode of Administration : To be applied on the head.

Therapeutic Uses : Cures dandruff & hair fall; also instantaneously cures psoriasis and boils as well as pimples on the head when applied.

(30) SIMPLE & EASY HOME REMEDY FOR THE CURE OF DANDRUFF

1.	**Pop borax**	**5 gms. (one teaspoon)**
2.	**Coconut oil**	**5 ml. (one teaspoon)**
3.	**Curd**	**15 ml. (3 teaspoon)**

Mode of Administration : Mix all these drugs together & apply in hair, wash after an hour. Also apply ***'Divya keśa taila'*** prepared in ashram, simultaneously.

Therapeutic Use : Cures dandruff immediately.

(31) HOME REMEDIES FOR URTICARIA

(A) 1.	**Coconut oil**	**50 ml.**
2.	**Camphor (native)**	**5 gms.**

Mode of Administration : Both of these drugs should be mixed together and applied over the rashes of urticaria.

Therapeutic Uses : Immediately cures urticaria, & removes burning sensation as well as itching.

(B) 1. *Marica* or black pepper — 5 in number
2. Brown sugar — 2 teaspoons (10 gms.)
3. Cow's ghee or pure ghee — 2 teaspoons (ml.)

Method of Preparation : Drugs nos. 2 and 3 should be ground well & mixed by adding no. 3 to make a paste.

Mode of Administration : This paste should be applied over affected parts two / three times per day.

Therapeutic Uses : Cures urticaria, leprosy and pruritus.

(32) HOME REMEDY FOR OBESITY

1. Powder of *Triphalā* — 1 teaspoon (5 gms.)
2. Water — 200 ml.

Method of Preparation : Drug no. 1 should be soaked in water (drug no. 2) during night. In the morning, this solution should be boiled till it is reduced to half and then strained out.

Mode of Administration : To be taken as hot as tolerable by adding two teaspoonfuls of honey.

Therapeutic Uses : Reduces lot of weight within few days.

(33) AŚVAGANDHĀ CŪRṆA : FOR WEAKNESS & EMACIATION

Powder of *Aśvagandhā* (*Withania somnifera*)

Dose : 1 teaspoon, twice a day.

Mode of Administration : To be taken in the morning & evening with milk .

Therapeutic Uses : Increases 3kg.–5kg. of weight within a month also cures weakness, diseases caused by the aggravation of *vāta* & nervous disorders.

(34) HOME REMEDIES FOR JAUNDICE

(A) 1. **Tender fresh leaves of Arka (*Calatropis procera*)**
2. **Betel-leaf**

Mode of Administration : Drug no. 1 should be made to a paste by grinding, kept in a betel-leaf and chewed. This process should be repeated for two/three days.

Therapeutic Uses : Cures jaundice & reduces the level of bilirubin (bile pigment) in the blood which is in excessive quantity.

(B) ***Viḍāla Ḍoḍā***

Mode of Administration : This drug should be soaked in the water during night. In the morning, former should be rubbed on a stone, & dropped 2/3 drops in the nostril or to be inhaled.

Therapeutic Uses : Cures jaundice.

(C) ***Dugdhikā*** **of Big Variety (*****Euphorbia hirta*****)**

Mode of Administration : This should be rubbed & taken internally.

Therapeutic Uses : Cures jaundice.

(35) GHTṚTA KUMĀRĪ (ALOE VERA) : PROMOTER OF PLATELATES

Pulp of ***Ghṛta-kumārī*** **(*****Aloe vera*****)**

Dose : 25-50 gms.

Mode of Administration : To be taken on empty stomach in the morning.

Therapeutic Uses : Promotes the quantity of reduced platelates, cures all types of abdominal disorders & female diseases. It also helps in curing diseases caused by the aggravation of *vāta,* thalassemea, Hapetitis 'B', constipation, flatulence, anorexia, nausea, burning sensation in the abdomen after having meal , irregular menstruation, burning sensation in micturition & dysuria.

(36) HOME REMEDY FOR HELMINTHES

(A) Juice of Leaves of Peach

Dose : 1 teaspoonful.

Mode of Administration : To be taken on empty stomach in the morning, regularly for 4/5 days.

Therapeutic Uses : Different types of intestinal worms come out within 4-5 days.

(B) Juice of the Leaves of *Marubaka* (*Majorana hortensis*)

Dose : 1 teaspoonful.

Mode of Administration : Leaves of *marubaka* (sweet marjoram) should be ground and juice is to be squeezed out. This should be taken on empty stomach in the morning. Alternatively, these leaves should be ground & made to a paste (chutney). To it, one gm. of *kampillaka* (*Mallotus philippinensis*) powder should be added and taken on empty stomach.

Therapeutic Uses : Different types of intestinal worms come out after dying.

(37) HOME REMEDY FOR EARACHE

Leaves of *Sudarśana* (*Crinum latifolium*)

Mode of Administration : These leaves should be made to a paste and juice should be squeezed out. This juice should be made luke-warm and two drops should be dropped in each ear twice/thrice a day.

Therapeutic Uses : Relieves earache immediately.

(38) HOME REMEDIES FOR CONSTIPATION

(A) Apple

Mode of Administration : One apple should be taken along with breakfast and dinner daily.

Therapeutic Uses : Cures constipation.

(B) Juice of Gourd

Dose : One cup.

Mode of Administration : To be taken in the morning on empty stomach.

Therapeutic Uses : Cleans the bowels well & cures as well as protects from all types of abdominal disorders.

(C) Papaya

If taken regularly, it protects the person from constipation.

(D) Pulp of *Āragvandha* or Purging cassia (*Cassia fistula*)

Dose : 10 – 20 gms.

(39) BILVA-CŪRṆA POWDER OF AEGLE MARMELOS : USEFUL IN TOXIC BYPRODUCT & CHRONIC SPRUE SYNDROME

Powder of *Bilva* (*Aegle marmelos*) – 1 teaspoonful

Or

Juice of *Bilva* – 1 glass (one dose)

Mode of Administration : To be taken twice daily, in the morning and evening.

Therapeutic Uses : Cures *āma* (toxic by product) caused by impaired digestion & metabolism, and binds excreta.

(40) LEAVES OF VĀSĀ (ADHATODA VASICA) : USEFUL IN COUGHING

1.	**Juice of the leaves of *Vāsā* (*Adhatoda vascia*)**	**1 teaspoon**	One dose
2.	**Juice of ginger**	**1 teaspoon**	
3.	**Honey**	**1 teaspoon**	

Mode of Administration : All of these three drugs should be mixed together and taken internally 2-3 times per day.

Therapeutic Uses : Cures all types of cough.

(41) HOME REMEDIES FOR COLD, CORYZA & FEVER

(A) 1.	**Leaves of *Tulasī* or holy basil (*Ocimum sanctum*)**	**7 leaves**	One dose
2.	**Clove**	**5 in number**	

Method of Preparation : Both of the above drugs should be made to pieces & boiled with water till half of it remains.

Mode of Administration : The above mentioned decoction should be taken internally by adding a little quantity of rock-salt. After taking this, one should lie down by covering his body with a cloth for fomentation. It should be taken twice / thrice per day for two or three days regularly.

Therapeutic Uses : Cures fever immediately, also useful in cold, coryza (catarrh) & cough.

(B) 1. Juice of *Tulasī* (*Ocimum sanctum*) 3– 4 drops] One dose
2. Juice of ginger 2– 3 drops]

Mode of Administration : Both of these drugs should be given to small children by adding honey to be licked.

Therapeutic Uses : Cures cold, catarrh and cough.

Note : It can also be given to newly born child in smaller dose.

(42) PIPPALĪ-KALPA FOR KAPHA PHLEGM & ASTHMA

Mode of Administration : On first day, one *pippalī* (*Piper longum*) should be boiled with cow's milk for 10 to 15 minutes. Then *pippalī* should be taken internally follwed by this milk. On next day, 2 *pippalīs* should be boiled with cow's milk as montioned above. Then *pippalīs* should be taken followed by milk. Like this, every day number of *pippalīs* should be increased one by one till the number of *pippalīs* reaches upto seven or eleven. If one does not feel warmth, then he can increase the number of *pippalīs* upto fifteen. If one feels warmth then he should stop increasing the number either at seven or at eleven. Thereafter, the number of *pippalīs* should be decreased gradually one by one every day till it reaches to one. This *pippalī*, followed by milk should be taken in the morning on empty stomach.

Therapeutic Uses : Cures phlegm, asthma, catarrh, cold & chronic cough. It is also useful in curing suppression of the power of digestion indigestion & wind formation (gas) in the stomach.

Note : The user of this *kalpa* should take simple & light food

Precaution : Avoid ghee (clarified butter), oil & sour as well as cold things.

(43) HOME REMEDY FOR GANGERENE

1. **Cow's ghee**
2. **Leaves of *vidhārā* (*Pueraria tuberosa*)**

Mode of Administration : Drug no. 1, i.e. cow's ghee should be applied over affected part. Then drug no. 2 should be tied over it.

Therapeutic Uses : Cures acute type of ulcer like gangerene within few days.

(44) HOME REMEDY FOR PROMOTION OF EYE-SIGHT

1.	**Rose - water**	**100 ml.**
2.	**Pulp of *Āmalakī* (*Emblica officinalis*)**	**10 gms.**

Method of Preparation : Drug no. 2 should be soaked in drug no.1 for two days. After two days, liquid should be decanted, filtered through eight-fold clean cloth and stored in a bottle.

Mode of Administration : 2-3 drops should be dropped in each eye.

Therapeutic Uses : Cures lachrymation & redness, burning as well as itching of eyes. Promotes eye sight.

(45) HOME REMEDY FOR CRACKED LIPS

Mustard Oil

Mode of Administration : To be applied daily in the navel after having shower.

Therapentic Uses : Cures cracked lips, removed dryness of face and promotes lustre.

(46) INHALATION : USEFUL IN HEADACHE, INSOMNIA & MIGRAINE PAIN

Almond Oil

Mode of Administration : 5 drops in each nostril should be deeply inhaled in the morning on empty stomach and at bed time.

Therapeutic Uses : Cures headache, migraine pain, insomnia, loss of memory, heavyness in the head, paralysis, parkinsonism, depression and sinusitis. It immediately relieves headache & sleeplessness.

Note : Head massage with almond oil is also very useful in all diseases mentioned above.

(47) LEAVES OF SADĀBAHĀR (LOCHNERA ROSEA) & HĀRASIṄGĀRA (NYCTANTHES ARBOR-TRISTIS) : USEFUL IN SCIATICA & DIABETES MELLITUS

(A) Leaves & flowers of *Sadābahāra* (*Lochnera rosea*) - 5 in number

Mode of Administration : To be taken regularly in the morning on empty stomach.

Therapeutic Uses : Controls the level of sugar (diabetes) and cures sciatica pain.

(B) Leaves or Flowers, or both of *Hārasingāra* (*Nyctanthes arbor-tristis*) - 5 in number

Mode of Administration : To be taken as such or should be made to a decotion and taken internally.

Therapeutic Uses : Controls diabetes and cures pain of sciatica.

(48) OINTMENT FOR VIPĀDIKĀ (CRACKS OF HEAL)

1. Mustard oil	**50 ml.**
2. Wax (native)	**25 gms.**
3. Camphor (native)	**5 gms.**

Method of Preparation : Heat the drug no. 1, i.e. mustard oil. When it starts boiling, drug no. 2., i.e. wax should be added to it slowly. When wax melts well and dissolves in the oil, then heat should be discontinued and mixture should be kept to be cooled. To this, drug no. 3., i.e. camphor should be added when it is luke-warm. Now ointment is ready.

Mode of Administration : Ointment should be applied in cracks of heal before going to bed.

Therapeutic Use : Relieves cracks of heals quickly from very first day of application.

(49) HOME REMEDIES FOR LEUCODERMA & SKIN-DISEASES

(A) 1. Cow's urine	**100ml.**
2. Neem leaf	**100gms.**
3. Juice of Cow-dung	**100gms.**
4. Powder of *Bākucī* (*Psoralia corylifolia*)	**100gms.**

Method of Preparation : All these four drugs should be mixed, ground and made to a paste.

Mode of Administration : To be applied externally on the affected parts of the body.

Therapeutic Uses : Cures leucoderma and other different types of skin-diseases.

(B)1. Root of *Punarnavā* (*Boerhavia diffusa*)
2. Bark of *Arjuna* (*Terminalia arjuna*)
3. Cow's urine

Method of Preparation : drug nos. 1 & 2 should be taken in equal quantity and made to a paste by adding cow's urine (drug no. 3).

Mode of Administration : To be applied externally.

Therapeutic Uses : Cures leucoderma.

(50) HOME REMEDY FOR STOMATITIS (INFLAMMATION OF MUCOUS LINING OF MOUTH)

(A)1. Copper sulphate (*Cupri sulphas*) 10 gms.
2. *Sphaṭika* (alum) 10 gms.

Method of Preparation : Both of these drugs should be roasted in a pan separately. Drug no. 1 (copper sulphate) should be half roasted (when it become half blue it should be taken out from the pan). Care should be taken that smoke, which comes out while roasting it, is not exposed to the eyes. Now pop alum & roasted copper sulphate should be mixed together.

Mode of Administration : One gm. of this mixture should be dissolved in one teaspoon of water, cotton should be soaked in this water and kept inside the mouth on affected part for one or two minutes. While applying this, one should be very careful that water coming out after its application should always be spit out, never be swallowed in. The water should be spit out till ten minutes after applying the medicine. Thereafter, mouth should be cleansed by gargling with clean water. If inflammation does not subside with this solution, then ash as such may be applied. Generally, this problem gets cured for ever, only with first application of this medicine, but if needed this can be repeated. The best time for its application is the morning on empty stomach or four hours after meal.

Note : After the application of this medicine taste of mouth becomes abnormal, which again becomes normal within one day.

(B) 1. Leaf of Common jasmine (*Jasmimum officinale*) 5 leaves
2. Leaf of Guava (*Psidium guajava*) 5 leaves

Mode of Administration : Both of these leaves should be chewed slowly for some time. After some time, water should be spit out.

Therapeutic Use : Cures stomatitis.

(51) MEDICINES FOR MOLES

(A) ***Divya Kāyā-kalpa Vaṭī* – 40 gms.**

Dose : 2 tabs. twice a day.

Mode of Administration : To be taken on empty stomach in the morning & evening with water.

(B) ***Divya Kaiśora Guggulu*** **- 40 gms.**

Dose : 1 tab. twice a day.

Mode of Administration : To be taken after lunch & dinner with water.

(52) HOME REMEDY FOR WARTS & CORNS

1.	**Lime (eatable)**	**10 gms.**
2.	***Sarjīkṣāra*** **(Sodium bicarbonate)**	**10 gms.**
3.	**Washing Soda**	**10 gms.**
4.	***Gairika*** **(Red ochre)**	**2 gms.**

Method of Preparation : All these four drugs should be mixed together, ground and made into an ointment by adding a little quantity of water.

Mode of Administration : This ointment should be applied only once on the warts with the help of matchstick or with cotton bud.

Therapeutic Use : Wart gets dried even by first application.

Note :

i) If wart does not get dried up by the first application, then process may be repeated once / twice at the interval of two / three days.

ii) This ointment should be applied very carefully.

For Corns :

Mode of Administration : Corn in the feet should be cut with help of a sharp instrument & thereafter, above mentioned ointment should be filled up therein. The process should be repeated for some days continuously.

Therapeutic Use : Removes corns.

(53) HOME REMEDY FOR NIGHT BLINDNESS & HYSTERIA

1.	**Juice of White onion**	**10 ml.**
2.	**Honey**	**10 ml.**

Mode of Administration : Both of these drugs should be mixed together and 2 drops should be dropped in each eye.

Therapeutic Uses : Cures night blindness & hysteria.

***

CHAPTER - V
WHOLESOME & UNWHOLESOME DIET, ETC. FOR DIFFERENT DISEASES

(1) HEART - DISEASES, HIGH BLOOD PRESSURE & HYPER TENSION

Wholesome : Wheat flour, Bajra (Pearl millet or *Pennisetum typhoides*) & Great millet (*Sorghum vulgare*) in small quantity, green gram (*Moong dal-Phaseolus mungo*), sprouted pulses, gram (*Cicer arietinum*), green leafy vegetables (spinach or *Spinacia oleracia, bathua*-Lamb's quarters or *Chenopodium murale*, green leaves of *methī*-Fenugreek or *Trigonella foenum-graecum*), parsle or *Trachyspermum ammi*, raisins, ginger, lemon, gourd, leaves of Holy basil or *Ocimum sanctum*, sweet luffa (*tori*) or *Luffa acutangula*, mint-leaf, *paṭola*-Pointed gourd or *Trichosanthes dioica*, drum stick or *Moringa oleifera, Lagenaria siceraria, tiṇḍa* or *Citrullus vulgaris, kāravella* (bitter gourd) or *Momordica charantia* are useful.

Grapes, mausammi (Sweet orange or *Citrus sinensis)*, papaya, pomegranate, orange, apple, guava, pine-apple, almond, milk without cream (fat), butter-milk, milk boiled with bark of *arjuna* (*Terminalia arjuna*), oils of mustard, sunflower & soya, cow's ghee, sugar, jaggery, honey, chutney etc. are also useful.

Unwholesome : Avoid cake, pastry, naun, *rhumāli roṭī,* noodles, pizza, burger, salt, fried food, packed & junk food, butter, ghee, *khoya* (condensed milk), milk-cream, flesh (meat), fish, food prepared with vegetable ghee (*dalda*), fried food prepared with fine flour (maida) & gram flour (*besan*), heavy food, jack fruit (*Artocarpus integra*), cashew nut, chest nut, pistachio (*Pistacia vera*) and other dry fruits, alcoholic drinks, pickle, sauce, fried papad, buiscuts, chips, smoking, etc.

Special Recommendation :

1. Take only whole grains & pulses.
2. Do light exercise & walk regularly. Don't exercise & walk immediate after taking meals.
3. Instead of taking fatty and heavy food together one should take light food in small intervals of time.
4. If patient is suffering from cough, then he should avoid yoghurt (curd), unripe banana and tomato. Take milk by adding ***Divya peya***.

(2) DIABETES MELLITUS

Wholesome : *Missa ata* i.e. flour prepared with wheat + barley + gram + soyabeen along with chalf, *moong, arhar* & gram *dal*,

Vegetables : Bitter gourd, pointed gourd, sweet luffa or *tori* (*Luffa acutangula*), gourd, tomato, cucumber, green chilli, spinach, *bathua* (Lamb's quarters or *Chenopodium murale)*, onion, garlic, lemon, fenugreek and drum stick; *āmalakī* (*Emblica officinalis*), fruit of jamun (black berry), powder of jamun-seed, water of fenugreek-seed, 5-7 tender leaves of neem (daily), fruits like papaya, guava, etc. in small quantity, milk without sugar, butter-milk, fruits having astringent taste in predomidance, should be taken. One should walk for 15-20 minutes after taking meals and a 3-4 km. walk daily is very useful.

Unwholesome : The Patient suffering from diabetes mellitus should avoid remain sitting or taking rest for a long time, sleep during day time after lunch, intake of freshly harvested grains, rice, curd, sugar-cane-juice, mausammi (sweet orange), banana, pomegranate, fig, cheeku, apple, sugar, jaggery, mishri (candied sugar) and potato. Smoking and alcohol aggravate the disease. One should never suppress the urges for urine and faeces.

(3) DIARRHOEA, DYSENTERY, SPRUE & IRRITABLE BOWEL SYNDROMES

Wholesome : One should take *daliyā* (mash) prepared with the equal quantities of wheat + rice + millet + moong, goat's milk, butter-milk (whey), ripe banana, fruit of bel, jam of *āmalaka* (*Emblica officinalis*), green coconut water, mint, *khichari*, curd (yoghurt), solution of lemon + salt + sugar, jam of bel, pulses of *moong* & lentil (*masoor*), parched rice, fried paddy, curd + isabagol husk, soup of gourd, sweet luffa or *Luffa acutangula* (*torī*), *tiṇḍā* (*Citrullus vulgaris*), etc., *Kūṣmāṇḍa Khaṇḍa, Nārikela Khaṇḍa* & fruit-juice. These are very useful.

Unwholesome : One should avoid fried food, like *poori*, *kachauri*, *samosa*, paties, food prepared with *urad dal* or black gram (*Phaseolus radiatus*), chana (gram) & fine flour (maida), chat, pickle, salt in large quantity, spicy food, sweets, yellow pumpkin, *karkaṭī* (*kakarī-Cucumis melo*), tomato, potato, leafy vegetables, milk, cold drinks, pizza, burger, etc.

(4) ACIDITY

Wholesome : *Chapati* or bread prepared with *missa atta* (flour prepared with wheat + barley + gram + soyabean with chaff), fiberous, leafy & green vegetables, gourd, sweet luffa or *torai* (*Luffa acutangula*), pointed gourd (paraval-*Trichosanthes dioica*), pumpkin, drum stick, bean (*sem*), fruit of *chaulai*, salad, sprouted grains, intake of laxative like *triphalā* + Isabagol husk with warm milk / water once a week, *daliyā* (gruel), *Khichari*, fresh whey, pomegranate, dry grapes, *gulakand*, raisins (*munakka*), *moong dal*, sweet & cold things, sweet of *petha*, jam of *amala* & apple are very useful.

Unwholesome : Avoid fried food (like *poori, halwa, kachauri, samosa*), pizza, burger, Idali, dosa, tea, coffee, cold drinks, *urad dal*, *rajamah* cow-pea-*Vigna unguiculata*, gram, *masoor dal* (lentil), hot spices, rice, amachur (powder of dry green mango), brinjal, potato, cauli flower, suran (*jamikanda* or *Amorphophallus campanulatus*), pickle, oily food, dishes prepared with *maida* (fine flour), *besan* (gram flour) & urad dal, red chilli, sharp food, heavy food, brinjal, *kulattha* (*Dolichos biflorus*), curd, smoking, alcoholic drinks and intake of hot food in haste and mental tension.

Note : For the patients suffering from piles, constipation, wind located in abdomem & other abdominal diseases, intake of ginger, lemon & different types of salt is useful.

(5) ANAEMEA, JAUNDICE, HEPATITIS A.B.C., HAEMATOLOGICAL DISORDERS, HEPATO SPLENOMEGALY

Wholesome : Barley, wheat, *missi chapati* of gram, *khichari, daliyā* (gruel), green leafy vegetables (spinach, fenugreek leaf-*methī*, *bathua*), gourd, *torai* or sweet luffa (*Luffa acutangula*), *ghṛta kumārī* (Aloe-*Aloe vera*), *tinda* or *Citrullus vulgaris*, pumpkin, *paṭola* or pointed gourd (*Trichosanthes dioica*), *chaulai* (*Amaranthus spinosus*), tender radish, papaya, *mausammi* (sweet orange), pomegranate, apple, orange, litchi (*Litchi chinensis*), *baggugosha* (var. of pear), grapes, green coconut-water, sugar, *mishri* (condied sugar), *āmalaka* (*Emblica officinalis*), dates, dry raisins, dry grapes, goat's milk, cow's milk, fresh curd, butter-milk, *rasa gulla* (type of sweet meat prepared with cheese and sugar), chewing of sugar-cane, sugar-cane juice are useful.

Unwholesome : Avoid hot spices, chillies, oil, sweet-meats, fatty food, *poori, parantha*, ghee (clarified butter), potato, rice, turmeric, milk with cream, yellow things, *kulattha* (*Dolichos biflorus*), mustard, garlic, *halwa, kachauri, samosa*, pizza, burger, tea, coffee, cold drinks, *urad dal* (black gram), *rajama* (cow pea – *Vigna unguiculata*), gram, masoor dal, junk & packed food which are being popular in the modern generation of today.

(6) OSTEO-ARTHRITIS, RHEUMATOID ARTHRITIS, GOUT, SCIATICA, SKELETAL & MUSCULAR PAIN, & FACIAL PARALYSIS, VĀTAJA-ROGAS (DISEASES CAUSED BY THE AGGRAVATION OF VĀTA)

Wholesome : Intake of chapati or bread prepared with wheat flour, *halwa* prepared by adding ghee & sugar, administration of external & internal oleation, vegetable prepared with the leaves of *punarnavā* (*Boerhavia diffusa*), pomegranate, ripe & sweet mango, grapes, castor oil, *moong dal*, asafoetida, ginger, dry ginger, fenugreek seed, *ajavayan* or parsle (*Trachyspermum ammi*), garlic, vegetable prepared of the flowers of drumstick tree and tender drumsticks, turmeric, use of *Aloe vera*, intake of hot water, shower with hot water and residing in warm environment is beneficial. Fomentation with hot water added with plenty of salt is very useful for a part affected with pain and oedema (inflammation).

Unwholesome : Intake of gram, pea, soyabean, potato, black gram (*urad dal*), cow-pea (*rajama-Vigna unguiculata*), jack-fruit, *masoor dal* (lentil), cauli-flower, cucumber, tomato, powder of green mango (*amchoor*), lemon, orange, grapes, curd, butter-milk, other sour things, buffalo's milk, white pumpkin and cold water, shower with cold water and residing in a moist and cold place are harmful. So all these should be avoided.

(7) CHRONIC RHINITIS, BRONCHITIS, BRONCHIAL ASTHMA, RTI, RESPIRATORY & ALLERGIC DISORDERS

Wholesome : Intake of barley, wheat, *moong dal* (green gram), horse gram (*kulatthī*), brinjal, goat's milk, dry raisins, clove, cardamom, garlic, *trikaṭu* (combination of dry ginger, long pepper & black pepper), long pepper, cassia (*tejapatra*), cinnamon, mace (*jāvitrī*) and roasted gram, chewing of black pepper & *mulethī* (Glycyrrhiza), intake of milk boiled with two gms. each (according to the constitution of body) of turmeric and dry ginger, and boiled by adding dates, dry dates and raisins are very useful.

Unwholesome : Avoid intake of *kheer* (food preparation prepared with milk & rice), curd, mustard, ice-cream, cold water of freez, cold drinks, fast food, junk food, sour thing, citrus fruits (lemon, orange, etc.), fried food, tamarind and pickle, exposure to cold wind, cold water, dust, pollen grains and smoke, as well as residing in moist, polluted & impure atmosphere.

(8) OBESITY

Wholesome : Intake of light & digestive food, cow's milk in less quantity and warm water added with honey + lemon in the morning, physical exercise, morning walk, physical as well as mental exertion are very useful. Also follow the general rules of prescriptions & prohibitions as mentioned on page no. 75.

Unwholesome : Avoid the intake of all types of fats and their preparations, and heavy as well as sweet things, sleep after food during day-time, eating in excessive quantity under the quench of taste and laziness.

(9) KIDNEY-DISEASES

Wholesome : Butter-milk prepared with cow's milk, fresh curd in less quantity, cow's milk, white pumpkin, *kakarī* (*Cucumis melo*), pointed gourd (*paraval*), coriander, aniseed (*saunf*), *punarnavā* (*Boerhavia diffusa*), papaya, apple, guava, sweet mango, *nāga kesara* (mesua or *Mesua ferrea*), gourd, *torai* or sweet tuffa (*Luffa acutangula*), *tiṇḍā* (*Citrullus vulgaris*), unripe papaya, banana, *sem-phali* (beans), drum stick, carrot, green coconut water, barley water, juice of pine-apple, leaves of *pāṣāṇabheda* or *pattharacaṭṭā* (*Bergenia ligulata*) & boiled water for drinking are useful.

Unwholesome : Peas, gram, *rajama* (cow peas-*Vigna unguiculata*), *urad dal* (black gram – *Phaseolus radiatus*), potato, cauli-flower, spinach, tomato, *chaulai* (*Amaranthus spinosus*), brinjal, mushroom, cheeku, ginger, curd, cashew nuts, red & green chillies, sour things, salt, black things, meat & alcoholic drinks should not be taken. One should also avoid exercise in excess.

(10) RENAL CALCULUS / STONE

Wholesome : Chapati (bread) of *missa ata* with chalf, *moong dal*, horse gram, red gram (*arhar dal*), lemon, carrot, cucumber, *karkaṭī* or *kakarī* (*Cucumis melo*), gourd, sweet luffa or *torai* (*Luffa acutangula*), *tinda* (*Citrullus vulgaris*), *mausammi* (sweet orange), orange, bitter gourd, green coconut water, leaves of *pāṣāṇa-bheda* (*Bergenia ligulata*), banana, pine apple juice, dry ginger, coriander, mint & plenty of water & other liquids should be taken.

Unwholesome : Cauli-flower, pumpkin, mushroom, brinjal, sour & salty things, spinach, cheese, tomato, *chaulai* (*Amaranthus spinosus*), *āmalaka*, seeds, fruits & vegetables having black colour, cheeku, cashew nuts, *kakarī* (*Cucumis melo*), cucumber, onion, black grapes, ingredients containing phosphorus & calcium, peas, different types of pulses (*dals*) and meat should not be taken.

(11) GYNAECOLOGICAL DISORDERS

Wholesome : As prescribed in general.

Unwholesome : Avoid sour things, hot spices, pickle, salt in large quantity, rice, *urad dal* (black gram), *rajma* (cow-peas-*Vigna unguiculata*), jack-fruit, potato, *jamikand* (*Amorphophallus campanulatus*), *ratālu* (var. of *Dioscorea eseulenta*), gram flour, food prepared from gram flour and fine flour (*maida*), oil and junk food popular in modern generation.

(12) SKIN-DISEASES

Wholesome : As prescribed in general.

Unwholesome : Intake of food having sour and saline tastes, brinjal, taro (*Colocasia esculenta*), *urad dal* (black gram), *rajma* (cow-peas – *Vigna unguiculata*), gram, fried food, food prepared with fine flour (*maida*) and gram flour, pickle, pizza, burger, paties, pastry, milk, curd, jaggery, sesame seed, garlic and hot spices, residing in very hot & moist place, use of soap, shampoo & cosmetics are prohibited.

(13) PAEDIATRIC DISEASES

Mother's milk and goat's / cow's milk are useful.

(14) PSYCHOLOGICAL DISEASES

Wholesome : Residing in a peaceful & calm place which is pleasing to one's mind, bathing, massage, positive thinking, emotional & moral support, meditation, regular practice of *prāṇāyāma* (breathing exercise), diet & regime which alleviate *vāta* (*vāyu*) & general prescriptions are useful.

Unwholesome : Intake of alcoholic drinks, mutually contradictory food, hot food & drinks, remaining hungry & thirsty, suppression of the urge for sleep, salt in excess, mustard oil, spices, pickle, intake of sharp & hot things, unfavourable environment, worry, fear, anger, grief, mental tension and remaining awake at night should be avoided.

(15) GENERAL PRESCRIPTIONS & PROHIBITIONS FOR ALL PATIENTS

Useful Ingredients : Intake of wheat, *moong dal* (with husk), gourd, sweet luffa or *torai* (*Luffa acutangula*), unripe papaya, carrot, *tinda* (*Citrullus vulgaris*), cabbage, bitter gourd, pointed gourd (*Trichosanthes dioica*), spinach, fenugreek leaf, sprouted grains, drumstick, black gram, less quantity of green chilli & ginger, cow's milk & ghee are useful in general. If cow's milk is not available, then buffalo's milk can be taken.

In fruits, apple, papaya, cheeku, pomegranate, guava, *baggugosha*, black berry and *mausammi* (sweet orange) are generally useful. In dry fruits, cashew nuts, almond, raisins, dry grapes, fig, chilgoza, pine (*Pinus gerardiana*), dates and dry dates can be taken.

Harmful Ingredients : Intake of tea, cold drinks, ice-cream, pizza, burger, paties, *idali*, *dosa*, tobacco, pouch (*guṭakhā*), *pan-masala*, meat, whisky & other alcoholic drinks, egg, food prepared with fine flour (*maida*) like bread etc., synthetic food, food from confectionary is harmful. One should never eat such things which are not eatable & which are prohibited.

MODE OF ADMINISTRATION OF MEDICINE IN GENERAL

1. **Tablets & Powder :** Tablets or pills and powders should be taken 15-20 minutes after the intake of meals. In the diseases caused by the aggravation of *vāta* and *kapha*, these should be taken with warm water, while in diseases caused by aggravated *pitta* these should be taken with fresh normal water. Tablets or pills taken by chewing produce better effects. If these are bitter in taste, then can be swallowed without chewing.

Note :

i) Take *Muktā-vaṭī, Madhunāśinī* (*Madhu-kalpa*) & *Kāyā-kalpa-vaṭī* one hour before taking meal followed by fresh water.

ii) Before taking the powders prescribed for diarrhoea and hyper-acidity, please consult the physician.

2. ***Bhasma* (Calcined powders) :** Mixture of *Bhasmas* (calcined powders) and *rasas* (mercury preparations) which is available in packets, should be taken half an hour before the meals along with honey, milk-cream or hot milk.

3. ***Āsavas & Ariṣṭas* :** All *Āsavas* & *Ariṣṭas* (self-fermented preparations) should be taken 10-15 minutes after the meal by adding equal quantity of water.

4. ***Kvātha* (Decoction) :** For decoction, 10 gms. of the medicine should be boiled with 400ml. of water till it is reduced to 100ml. and then filtered. If the patient is not able to take it in large dose, i.e 100 ml. then it can be boiled more and reduced to 50 ml. If decoction is bitter or pungent in taste, then honey, sugar or jaggery can be added to it. However, it is more effective without an addition of any sweetener as mentioned above. If medicine is soaked in water for 8-10 hours before boiling, it will be more effective & beneficial.

5. **Acupressure :** The pressure should be given with the help of thumb, etc. for 30-40 times on the mentioned points according to the disease. Pressure should be given before the intake of meal. Vital parts should be pressurized by applying moderate strength. This is a marvelous therapy to cure pain. Though painful in beginning, but is exceedingly beneficial in results.

6. **Massage :** Massage should be always done gently towards the heart by applying proper pressure.

7. **Steam-bath with Decoction (*Kvātha-snāna*)**

i) If one has to steam-bathe, then firstly medicine prescribed for that particular disease should be boiled in a pressure cooker by adding 1 ltr.-1½ ltrs. of water. The weight (whistle) of the cooker should be taken out when steam starts to come out. In the place of weight (whistle), the rubber pipe of gas should be fixed. Then affected part of the body should be fomented with the steam coming out from the other side of the pipe. It is advisable that a piece of cloth should be tied on this side so that very hot drops of water coming out along with steam may not burn the body. After taking steam for prescribed period, the remaining medicine (liquid) should be used for fomenting the painful part when it is moderately hot.

ii) If the patient doesn't like to take steam-bath, then the medicine should be boiled with 3-4 ltrs. of water till it is reduced to half. This tolerably warm liquid is to be used for fomenting the affected part with the help of a piece of cloth.

8. ***Yogāsanas & Prāṇāyāma* (Physical & Breathing Exercises) :** *Prāṇāyāma* (breathing exercise) produces marvelous effects on all types of curable and incurable diseases. It should be practised regularly on empty stomach according to one's own capacity and strength. In arthritis, practice of light exercises, and in the pains of lumbar region & spine, *āsanas* (exercises) prescribed for spinal chord are certainly beneficial.

***

APPENDIX – I

(Names of Medicines Described in the Text)	Ch. & Receip No.	Page No.
Divya Amṛta Rasāyana (Linctus)	I : 24	14
Divya Arśa-kalpa Vaṭī	I : 1	1
Divya Aśmarī-hara Kvātha	I : 2	1
Divya Aśmarī-hara Rasa	I : 3	2
Divya Aśmarī-hara Vaṭī	I : 4	2
Divya Bādāma Pāka	II : 7	24
Divya Candraprabhā Vaṭī	II : 5	22
Divya Cyavana Prāśa (Linctus)	II : 4	22
Divya Cūrṇa	I : 11	6
Divya Danta Mañjana	I : 14	7
Divya Dhārā	I : 13	7
Divya Gaisa-hara Cūrṇa	I : 10	5
Divya Hṛdayāmṛta Vaṭī	I : 28	16
Divya Kānti Lepa	I : 32	19
Divya Kāyā-kalpa Kvātha	I : 84	4
Divya Kāyā-kalpa Taila	I : 7	4
Divya Kāyā-kalpa Vaṭī	I : 6	3
Divya Keśa Taila	I : 9	5
Divya Madhu-kalpa Vaṭī	I : 20	11
Divya Madhunāśinī Vaṭī	I : 19	10
Divya Medhā Kvātha	I : 22	13
Divya Medhā Vaṭī	I : 23	13
Divya Medohara Vaṭī (Weightless)	I : 25	14
Divya Muktā Piṣṭī	II : 2	21
Divya Muktā Vaṭī	I : 21	11
Divya Peya (Herbal Tea)	I : 12	6
Divya Pīḍāntaka Kvātha	I : 16	8
Divya Pīḍāntaka Rasa	I : 15	8
Divya Pīḍāntaka Taila	I : 17	9

APPENDIX -II

BOTANICAL / ENG. EQUIVALENTS OF THE NAME OF THE DRUGS USED IN RECIPES (GIVEN IN SKT. / HINDI / FOLK LANGUAGES)

NAMES OF DRUGS	BOTANICAL / ENG. NAMES	CH. & ITEM NO.	Page No.
Abhraka bhasma	Calcined powder of mica	I : 26	15
Ajamodā (Ajavayan)	*Trachyspermum ammi*	I : 4,10,13,15-17	2,5,7,8,9
Ākārakarabha (Akarakara)	*Anacyclus pyrethrum*	I : 14,18,26; IV:3	7,10,15,49
Akīka piṣṭī	n. of a med. prepared with agate	I : 28	16
Āmalaka(ī) (amala)	*Emblica officinalis*	I:4,7,9,24,25,27,30; IV:44	2,4,5,14,14,16,18,68
Ambara-dhāna	?	I : 27	16
Āmra	*Mangifera indica*	I : 4	2
Āmragandhi haridrā (Amba haldi)	*Curcuma amada*	I : 37	
Amṛtā	*Tinospora cordifolia*	I : 6-8, 12, 19, 28	3,4,6,10,16
Ananta-mūla	root of *Fagonia cretica*	I : 9	5
Apāmārga	*Achyranthes aspera*	IV: 19	56
Āragvadha (Amaltas)	*Cassia fistula*	I : 31; IV:38	18,65
Araṇya jīraka (Kali jiri)	*Centratherum anthelminticum*	1 : 6,7,19; IV:22	3,4,10,58
Ariṣṭaka (Ritha)	*Sapindus trifoliatus* (soap-nut)	1 : 1	1
Arjuna	*Terminalia arjuna*	1 : 12,20,28; IV:5,50	6,11,16,50,70
Arka	*Calotropis procera*	I : 17; IV:34	9,63
Aśoka	*Saraca asoca*	I : 27	16
Aśvagandhā	*Withania somnifera*	I : 12,15,16,19,21-23, 27, 28-30; IV:18, 21, 34	6,8,8,10,11,13 16,16,18,55,58,63
Aśvattha (Pīpala)	*Ficus religiosa*	IV : 15	54
Ativiṣā (Atis)	*Aconitum heterophilum*	I : 4, 19	2,10
Ātmaguptā (Māla-kaṅganī)	*Mucuna pruriens*	I : 18	10
Babbūla	*Acacia arabica*	I : 14, 19; IV : 3	7,10,49
Bākucī (Bavachi)	*Psoralia corylifolia*	I : 6-8; IV : 50	3,4,70
Bakula (Maulasiri)	*Mimusops elengi*	I : 14	7
Balā	*Sida cordifolia*	I : 9, 18	5,10
Banaphśā	*Viola odorata*	I : 12	6
Bhṛṅga-rāja	*Eclipta alba*	I : 9, 17	5,9
Bhūmyāmalakī (bhūmi āmalā)	*Phyllanthus niruri*	1 : 4, 12, 30,31; IV:6	2,6,18, 8,51
Bibhītaka (baheda)	*Terminalia belerica*	I : 4, 25; IV:3, 16	2,14,49,55
Bījabanda (seed of *Balā*)	seed of *Sida cordifolia*	I : 27	16

Bilva	*Aegle marmelos*	I : 4,19; IV:3, 16; IV:39	2,10,49,55,66
Brāhmī	*Bacopa monnieri* or *Centella asiatica*	I : 9,12,21-24	5,6,11,14
Cakra-marda (Panvad)	*Cassia tora*	I : 6-8	3,4
Candana	*Pterocarpus santalinus*	I: 12	6
Candana (śveta)	*Santalum album*	I :6-8,9,12,32	3,4,5,6,19
Cavya	*Piper chaba*	I : 12	6
Citraka	*Plumbago zeylanica*	I : 4,12,17,28	2,6,9,16
Dama bela	*Tilophor indica*	IV : 43	67
Dāru-haridrā	*Berberis aristata*	I : 6-8, 9,17,27	3,4,5,9,16
Daśa-mūla	a collective n. for the roots of ten drugs viz., *bilva, śyonāka, gambhāri, pāṭalā, gaṇikārikā, śālaparṇī, pṛśniparṇī, bṛhatī, kaṇṭakārī & gokṣura*	1:15,17	8,9
Deva-dāru	*Cetrus deodara*	1:6-8, 27	3,4,16
Dhattūra	*Datura metel*	I : 17	9
Droṇa-puṣpī	*Leucas cephalotes*	I : 6-8	3,4
Dugdhikā (big var.)	*Euphorbia hirta*	IV : 34	63
Elā	*Elettaria cardamomum*	I : 12, 24	6,14
Eraṇḍa, root	*Ricinus communis*	I : 16,17	8,9
Gairika	red ochre	IV : 52	71
Gaja pippalī	fruit of *Piper chaba*	I : 16,17	8,9
Gandha-prasāraṇī	*Paderia foetida*	I : 17	9
Ghṛta kumārī (Aloe)	*Aloe vera*	I : 1,4; IV : 35	1,2,64
Godantī bhasma	calcined powder of gypsum	I : 26	15
Go-jihvā (Gājabān)	*Onosma bracteatum*	I : 21	13
Gokṣura	*Tribulus trrestris*	I : 2,19	1,10
Guḍamāra (Meṣa śṛṅgī)	*Gymnema sylvestra*	I : 19	10
Guḍūcī	*Tinospora cordifolia*	IV : 14,22	54,58
Guggulu (pure)	*Commiphora mukul*	I : 25, 27, 28	14,16,16
Guñjā (rattī-white var.)	*Abrus precatorius,* white var.	I : 9	5
Hajarala yahūda	?	I : 3	2
Hārasiṅgāra (pārijāta)	*Nyctanthes arbortristis*	IV : 48	69
Haridrā (Haldi)	*Curcuma longa* (turmeric)	I : 6-8, 19,32; IV : 3,18	3,4,10,19,49,55
Harītakī (Jaṅgh harad)	*Terminalia chebula*	I : 1,6,7,25	1,3,4,14
Hiṅgu	*Ferula foetida*	I : 10	5
Hīraka bhasma	calcined powder of diamond	I : 15,28	8,16
Indrāyaṇa (Indravāruṇī)	*Citrullus colocynthis*	I : 6	3
Jambū (Jamun)	*Syzygium cumini*	I : 19; IV : 22	10,58
Jaṅga harītakī	var. of *Terminalia chebula*	I : 10,11	5,6

Jatāmāṃsī	*Nardostachys jatamansi*	I : 9,17,21-23	5,9,11,13
Jātī-patrī	Mace or aril of *Myristica fragrance*	I : 12,18	6,10
Jātī phala	*Myristica fragrance*	I : 12,18,32	6,10,19
Jīraka	*Cuminum cyminum*	I : 9	5
Jīvaka	*Malaxis acuminate*	I : 17	9
Jūnde-bedastara	*Castorium* (beaver)	I ; 18	10
Jyotiṣmatī (Māla kaṅganī)	*Celatrus paniculatus*	I ; 17,21-23	9,11,13
Kākamācī (Makoy)	*Solanum nigrum*	I : 1,4,31	1,2,18
Kākolī	*Roscoea alpina*	I : 17	9
Kāla-megha	*Andrographis paniculata*	I : 19; IV : 22	10,58
Kamala	*Nelumbo nucifera*	I : 9,27	5,16
Kampillaka	*Mallotus philippinensis* (dye)	IV : 36	63
Kaṇṭakārī	*Solanum indicum*	I : 7	4
Kapardaka bhasma	calcined powder of *Cypraea moneta*	I : 27	16
Kapi-kacchū	*Mucuna prurita*	I : 24	14
Karañja	*Pongamia pinnata*	I : 6-8	3,4
Kāravellaka	*Momordica charantia*	I : 19; IV : 22	10,58
Karcūra	*Curcuma zedoaria*	I : 19	10
Karkaṭa śṛṅgī	*Pistacia integerrima*	I : 26	15
Karpūra (camphor)	*Cinnamomum camphora*	I : 1,13,14,32	1,7,7,19
Kāsīsa bhasma	calcined powder of iron sulphate	I : 4	2
Kaṭukī (Kuṭakī)	*Picrorhiza kurroa*	I : 4,6-8,19, 25-29; IV : 22	2,3,4,10,14,17 58
Keśara	*Crocus sativus*	I : 18,24	10,14
Ketakī	*Pandanus tectorius*	I : 9	5
Khadira	*Acacia catechu*	I : 6-8, 32	3,4,19
Revan(nd)a cīnī	*Rheum emodi*	I : 5	3
Khūna kharābā (Rakta-niryāsa)	*Daemenorops draco*	I : 1	1
Kirāta-tikta-ka (Chirayata)	*Swertia chirata*	I : 6-8, 19; IV : 22	3,4,10,58
Kṛṣṇa bīja (Kālā dānā)	*Ipomoea nil*	I : 11	6
Kṣīra-kākolī	*Lillium polyphyllum*	I : 17	9
Kulattha	*Dolichos biflorus*	I : 2	1
Kupīlu (pure)	*Strychnos nux-vomica*	I ; 15, 17	8,9
Kuṭaja	*Holarrhena antidysenteica*	I : 19	10
Laghu kaṇṭakārī	*Solanum xanthocarpum*	I : 6	3
Laśuna	*Allium sativum*	I : 17; IV : 18	9,55
Lauha bhasma	calcined powder of iron	I : 4	2
Lavaṅga	*Syzygium aromaticum*	I ; 12-14, 26; IV : 3	6,7,15,10,49
Lodhra	*Symplocos crataegoides*	I : 9	5
Madayantikā (Mehandi)	*Lawsonia inermis* (henna)	I : 32	19

Madhu yaṣṭī (Mulethi)	*Glycyrrhiza glabra*	I : 5,17,26,27	3,9,15,16
Mahā Vāta-vidhvaṃsana Rasa	n.of a classical medicine	I : 15	8
Makaradhvaja	n. of a classical med.	I : 18	10
Manaḥśilā	realgar	I : 26	15
Maṇḍūra bhasma	calcined powder of iron rust	I : 4,15	2,8
Mañjiṣṭhā	*Rubia cordifolia*	I : 6-8, 17,32	3,4,9,19
Marica	*Piper nigrum*	I : 10,12; IV : 17,31	5,6,55,62
Marubaka	*Majorana hortensis*	IV : 36	64
Māyāphala (Maju-phala)	*Quercus infectoria*	I : 14	7
Mayūra-piccha bhasma	calcined powder of feather of pea-cock	I : 27	16
Medā	*Polygonatum verticillatum*	I : 17	9
Methikā (Methī)	*Trigonella foenum-graecum*	I : 19,29; IV:18,22	10,17,55,58
Miśrī	sugar candy	I : 15	8
Miśreyā (Saunf)	*Foeniculum vulgare*	I : 5,11,12,17,21	3,6,6,9,11
Motī piṣṭī (Muktā piṣṭī)	n. of a classical medicine prepared with pearl	I : 15,21,23,28	8,11,13,16
Muktā-śukti bhasma	calcined powder of pearl-oyster	I : 4, 26	2,15
Mūlī kṣāra	alkaline preparation of *Raphanus sativus*	I : 3	2
Musta	*Cyperus rotundus*	I : 9,12,15,16,28; IV : 18	5,6,8,8,16,55
Nāga dauna (Nāga-damana)	*Artemisia vulgaris*	I : 1	1
Nāga keśara	*Mesua ferrea*	I : 9,17,27	5,9,16
Nīlinī	*Indigofera tinctoria*	I : 9	5
Nimba	*Azadirachta indica*	I : 6,7	3,4
Nimba, sweet var. *(Bakayan)*	*Melia azedarch*	I : 1	1
Nirguṇḍī	*Vitex negundo*	I : 15-17, 28	8,9,16
Palāśa	*Butea monosperma*	I : 17; IV: 18	9,55
Pārasa pīpala	?	I : 27	16
Pārijātaka	*Nyctanthes arbortristis*	I : 16	8
Pāsāṇa-bheda (Pattharacaṭṭā)	*Bergenia ligulata*	I : 2; IV : 24	1,60
Pepper mint	*Pepper mint*	I : 13,14	7,7
Pīpala (Aśvattha)	*Ficus religiosa*	IV : 25	60
Pippalī	*Piper longum*	I : 12,14,16,17; IV : 42	6,7,8,9,67
Pravāla piṣṭī	n. of a classical medicine	I : 15,23,24,27; IV : 16	8,13,14,16,55
Priyaṅgu	*Callicarpa macrophylla*	I : 9	5
Punarnavā	*Boerhaavia diffusa*	I:2,4,12,25,28,31; IV:6,50	1,2,6,14,16,18,51,70
Puṣkara mūla	*Inula racemosa*	I : 17,21-23	9,11,13

Putrajīvaka	*Putranjiva roxburghii*	IV : 19	56
Rajata bhasma	calcined powder of silver	I : 23,28	13,16
Rasāñjana (Rasaunt)	solid extract of *Berberis aristata*	I : 1	1
Rāsnā	*Pluchea lanceolata*	I : 15-17, 28	8,9,16
Ratanajota	*Onosma ehioides*	I : 9	5
Rohiṣa (Agiya ghas)	*Cymbopogon martini*	I : 12	6
Rudantī	*Capparis moonii*	I : 26	15
Samudra phena	cuttle fish	I : 32	19
Sadābahāra (flower)	*Lochnera rosea*	IV : 22,48	58,69
Saṅgeyaśada piṣṭī	n. of med. prepared with *Magnasium sallicate* or soap-stone	I : 28	16
Śaṅkha bhasma	calcined powder of conch-shell	I : 4	2
Śaṅkha-puṣpī	*Convovulus pluricaulis*	I ; 12,21-24	6,11,14
Sarja (kaharava)	*Vateria indica*	I ; 1	1
Sarjīkṣāra	Sodium bicarbonate	IV : 52	71
Sarpa-gandhā	*Rauwolfia serpentina*	I : 21	11
Śata-patrī (rose flower)	*Rosa centifolia*	I : 5	3
Śata-puṣpā	*Anethum sowa*	I ; 17	9
Śatāvarī (a)	*Asparagus racemosus*	I : 17,18,24,27; IV : 13	9,10,14,16,53
Śilājatu (śilājīta)	mineral pitch, bitumen	I : 15,19,27,30; II : 1	8,10,16,18,20
Śilājīta sat	extract of mineral pitch	I ; 25,28	14,16,
Śiṃśapā (Śīśama)	*Dalbergia sissoo*	III : 25; IV : 10	41,52
Śivaliṅgī seed	seed of *Bryonia laciniosa*	I : 27	16
Śobhāñjana (sweet var.)	*Moringa oleifera*	I : 15,29	8,16
Soma-latā	*Ephedre gerardiana*	I : 12	6
Sphaṭika	alum	IV : 3,51	49,71
Sphaṭika bhasma	calcined powder of alum	I : 14,26,32	7,15,19
Śṛṅga bhasma	calcined powder of horn of deer	I ; 26,28	15,16
Sudarśana	*Crinum latifolium*	IV : 37	65
Śuṇṭhī (dry ginger)	*Zingiber officinale*	I : 16,17,29; IV : 18	8,9,17,55
Svarṇa-bhasma	calcined powder of gold	I : 18	10
Svarṇa-mākṣika bhasma	calcined powder of Copper pyrite	I : 15	8
Svarṇa-patrī (Sanay)	*Cassia angustifolia*	I : 5,11	3,6
Śveta parpaṭī	n.of a kind of scale preparation	I : 3	2
Śyonāka (bark)	*Oroxylum indicum*	IV : 6	51
Tagara (Sugandha-bālā)	*Valeriana wallichii*	I : 17, 32	9,19
Ṭaṅkaṇa bhasma	calcined powder of borax	I : 26	15
Teja-patra	leaf of *Cinnamomum zeylanicum*	I : 12,17	6,9
Tila taila	oil extracted from the seeds of *Sesamum indicum* (sesame oil)	I : 7	4

Trikaṭu	a collective n. for *śuṇṭhī* or *Zingiber officinale, pippalī* or *Piper longum & marica* or *Piper nigrum*	I : 26; IV : 16,26	15,55,61
Triphalā	a collective n. for *harītakī* or *Terminalia chebula, bibhītaka* or *Terminalia belerica & āmalakī* or *Emblica officinalis*	I : 6,19,27,30; IV : 32	3,10,16,18,63
Trivṛt (Nishoth)	*Operculina turpethum*	I : 4,24	2,14
Tulasī	*Ocimum sanctum*	I : 12; IV : 4,41	6,50,66
Tumburu	*Zanthoxylum alatum*	I : 14; IV : 3	7,49
Tvak	*Cinnamomum zeylanicum*	I : 12,24,26	6,14,15
Uṣbā	*Sarsa parilla*	I : 6-8	3,4
Ustūkhūdūsa	*Lavandula stoechas* (Arabian or French Lavender)	I : 21-23	11,13
Vaca (ā)	*Acorus calamus*	I : 17,22,23	9,13,13
Vaṃśalocana	bamboo manna	I : 24	14
Varuṇa	*Crataeva nurvula*	I : 2	1
Vāsā	*Adhatoda vasica*	I : 12; IV : 40	6,66
Vaṭa-jaṭā	adventitious roots of *Ficus bengalensis*	I : 19	10
Vatsanābha	*Aconitum ferox*	I : 17,26	9,15
Viḍaṅga	*Embelia ribes*	I : 25	14
Vidhārā (Vidārī kanda)	*Pueraria tuberosa*	IV : 44	68
Vṛddhi	*Hebenaria intermedia*	I : 17	9
Yava-kṣāra	alkaline preparation of *Hordeum vulgare*	I : 3	2
Yogrāja guggulu	n. of a classical med. containing *guggulu* or *Commiphora mukul* in abundance	I : 15	8

APPENDIX III

Names of Diseases for which Medicines are Prescribed.

Disease	Ch. & Item No.	P. No.
(A)		
Abdomen, heaviness	I:10	5
Abdominal diseases	I:4, III : 4	2.26
Abdominal pain	I:4,10, 11,	2,5,6
Acidity	I:10, II:2, III:16	5,21,33
Acne	I : 6, 32	3,19
Vulgre	III:4	27
Aggravation of *pitta*	II:2	21
Alopecia	I:9	5
Āma (toxic byproduct due	I:5, III:14	3,32
(to impairement of digestion & metabolism)		
Āma-vāta (rheumatoid arthritis)	I:29	17
Amenorrhoea	III:25	41
Anaemia	I:4, II:5, 6	2,22,23
Angina pain	I:28	15
Anorexia	I:10, II:5	5,22
Anxiety	I:21	11
Arthritis	II:3,5	21,22
Asthma	I:13, 26; II:1,6; III:21,	7,15,20,23,37
	IV:26, 42,43	61,67,67
Aversion from food	II:2	21
(B)		
Bhagandara (fistula in-ano)	II:5	22
Bleeding (from nose, mouth & rectum	II:2	21
Bue to the exposure to strong sun)		
Bleeding piles	I:1, IV:8, 9	1,51,51
Blockage of arteries of heart	1:28	16
Blockage of heart	I:28	16
Blurred vision	I:19	10
Bodily pains	I:15	8
Bronchitis	I:26, II:1, 4,6	15,20,22,24
Burns	I:7	4
Burning sensation	I:1, 5; II:2	1,3,21
In all over the body		

In eyes	II:2	21
Head	II:2	21
Throat	II:2	21
Urethera	II:2	21
Urine	I:3	2

(C)

Calculi	I:3	2
Cancer	III:23, IV:14	38,54
Cardiac tonic	II:7	24
Cardiac weakness	II:7	24
Cataract	III:31, IV: 2	45,49
Cervical spondylitis	I:15,17; II:1,5; III:20	8,9,20,22,36
Cholera	I:13	7
Cholesterol	I:12, 21, 28	7,11,16
Chronic arthritis	II : 3	21
Chronic cough	IV:7	28
Disease	I:26	15
Fever	I:4	2
Headache	I:22	13
Renal failure	III:28	43
Rhinitis	III:21; IV: 26	37,61
Sprue syndrome	IV: 39	66
Cirrhosis of liver	II:27; IV: 6	21,51
Cold	I:2, 26; II:1; IV: 41	1,15,20,66
Colic pain	I:1, 10, 13; II:6	1,5,7,23
Constipation	I:4,5,11; III:33; IV:38	21
Consumption	II:2	72
Corns	IV:53	34
Coronary artery diseases	III:17	15,20,37,66
Coryza	I:26; II:1; III:21; IV:41	15,20,22,23,61,66
Cough, Coughing	I:26; II:1,4,6; IV: 26, 40	68
Cracked lips	IV: 46	4
Crackes of feet	I:7	4
Hand	I:7	69
Heals	IV:49	4
Cuts	I:7	

(D)

Dadru (ring-worm)	I:6, 7	3,4
Dandruff	I:9; IV:29, 30	5,62,62

(F)

Female diseases	I:27	16
Fever	II:2; IV:41	21,66
Chronic	I:4	2
Fibroid uterus	II:2,4	21,22
Filariasis	I:8	4
Flatulence	I:10,11,13; III:13	5,6,7,31
Foul smell of mouth	I:14	7
Freckles	I:7	4
Frequent urination	I:19	10

(G)

Galactagogue for mothers	IV:13	53
Gangerene	IV:44	68
Gas	I:10	5
Gas in abdomen	I:10, 13	5,7
Gastric trouble	III: 13	31
Giddiness	II:2,6	21,23
Glaucoma	III:31; IV:2	45,49
Gonorrhroea	II:5	22
Gout	I:16; II:1; III:19	8,20,35
Greying of hair	I:9; IV:. 27	5,61
Growth in body (any)	III:7	28
Growth of big size	III:8	28

(H)

Hair diseases	IV:28	61
Hair fall	I:9; IV: 27	5,61
Handicapped children	III:10	29
Harshness in speech	II:2	21
Headache	I:9, 13, II:2,7 III:18; IV:26,47	5,7,21,24,34,61,68
Head diseases	I:9	5
Heart diseases	I:11,12; IV: 4, 21	6,6,50,58
Heaviness of abdomen	I:10	5
Heaviness of head	I:26	15
Hepatitis	IV:6	51
A,B,C	III:26	41
B,C.	I:31	18
Hernia	III:29	44
heterogenous substances	II:3	21

Less of sleep	I:22	13
Leucoderma	I:6,7; III:5,	3,4,27
Leucorrhoea	I:27,30; II:6; IV:10	16,18,23,52
Liver diseases	I:4	2
Loss of appetite	I:31	18
Loss of lustre	I:32	19
memory	I:23; II:6	13,23
shining	I:32	19
weight	I:19	10
Lumbar pain	I:15; II:5	8,22

(M)

Madhumeha (diabetes mellitus)	IV:22	58
Malaria	II:3,	21
Menorrhagia	I:27; II:6; III:25; IV:10,11	16,23,41,52,53
Menstruation, excessive	II:5	22
Mental disorders	I:23	13
Mental retardation	III:11	30
Mental weakness	II:4	22
Migraine pain	I:22; III:18; IV: 47	13,34,68
Moles	IV:52	71
Mongoloid children	III:11	30
Morbid thirst	I:19; II:2	10,21
Multiple sclerosis	III:12	31
Muscular distrophy	III:10	29
Muscular pain	I:16	8
Mūtra kṛcchra (dysuria)	II:2,5	21,22

(N)

Nausea	I:11	6
Negative thinking	I:23	13
Negativity	I:22	13
Nervous weakness	I:3, 7	2,4
Night blindness	IV:53	72
Night emission by hand (*svapna doṣa*)	I:30	18
Normal delivery	IV:20	57
Nourishment of seven *dhātus* (tissue elements)	II:4	22
Numbness in hands & feet	I:19	10

(O)

Obesity	I:8; III : 1; IV:1, 21, 32	4,26,49,58,62

Stomatitis	IV:51	71
Stone in gall bladder	I:2	1
of kidney	I:7; IV:24	4,60
in urinary tract	I:2; II:5	1,22
Stone formation	I:3	2
Sun burn	I:7	4
Suppression of the power of digestion	I:4; II:5	2,22
Suppression of urination	II:5	22
Syphilis	II:5	22
(T)		
Testicle enlargement	II:5	22
Thalassemea	III:9	29
Thyroid	IV:16	55
disorders (hypo + hyper thyroid)	I:25	14
Tingling sensation	I:19	10
Tiredness	I:19	10
Tonic	I:24, 26	14,15
Tonsilitis	IV:16	55
Toothache	I:13	7
Tooth-diseases	I:13	7
Toxic byproduct	IV:39	66
Trauma	I:13, 17	7,9
Tuberculosis	II:1,3	20,21
Tumour	III:7	28
of big size	III:8	28
Tympanitis	III:36	48
(U)		
Uncomfort	II:2	21
Uneasiness	I:10,21,22,23,28	5,11,13,13,16
Urination, frequent	I:19	10
Urticaria	IV:31	62
(V)		
Vāta-roga (diseases caused by the vitiation of *vāta-doṣa*)	I:29; IV:18	17,55
Vipādikā (cracks of heals)	IV:49	69
Vitiated blood	II:3	21
(W)		
Warts	IV:53	72

RATE LIST OF SELF EXPERIENCE (PATENT) MEDICINES

Sr. No.	Name of Medcine	Quantity	Rates (Rs.)
1.	Divya Arshakalp Vati	20 g.	30/-
		40 g.	60/-
2.	Divya Ashmarihar Ras	50 g.	80/-
3.	Divya Ashmarihar Kvath	100 g.	20/-
4.	Divya Amala Murabba (Wet)	1 Kg.	70/-
5.	Divya Amala Murabba (Sweetened)	500 g.	70/-
6.	Divya Amala Murabba (Spicy)	500 g.	85/-
7.	Divya Udaramrit Vati	20 g.	25/-
		40 g.	50/-
8.	Divya Udarakalp Choorna	50 g.	15/-
		100 g.	30/-
9.	Divya Kayakalp Vati	10 g.	35/-
		20 g.	70/-
10.	Divya Kayakalp Tail	50 ml.	25/-
		100 ml.	50/-
		250 ml.	125/-
11.	Divya Kayakalp kvātha	100 g.	20/-
12.	Divya Kesh Taila	50 g.	35/-
		100 g.	70/-
		250 g.	175/-
13.	Divya Gaisahar Choorna	50 g.	20/-
		100 g.	40/-
14.	Divya Dadru Arka	10 ml.	15/-
15.	Divya Choorna	50 g.	20/-
		100 g.	40/-
16.	Divya Peya (Herbal Tea)	100 g.	20/-
		250 g.	50/-
		500 g.	100/-
		1 Kg.	200/-

17.	Divya Dhara	10 ml.	10/-
		20 ml.	20/-
18,.	Divya Danta Manjan	50 g.	20/-
		100 g.	40/-
19.	Divya Netra Jyoti	10 ml.	10/-
		20 ml.	20/-
20.	Divya Pidantak Ras	10 g.	40/-
		20 g.	80/-
21.	Divya Pidantak Kvath	100 g.	15/-
22.	Divya Pidantak Tail	50 ml.	30/-
		100 ml.	60/-
23.	Divya Paushtik Choorna	50 g.	15/-
		100 g.	30/-
24.	Divya Yauvanamrit Vati	5 g.	210/-
		10 g.	420/-
25.	Divya Madhu (Pure Honey)	250 g.	35/-
		1 Kg.	140/-
26.	Divya Madhunashini	20 g.	60/-
		60 g.	180/-
27.	Divya Mukta Vati	20 g.	100/-
		40 g.	200/-
28.	Divya Medha Kvath	100 g.	20/-
29.	Divya Medha Vati	20 g.	45/-
		60 g.	135/-
30.	Divya Amrit Rasayan (Linctus)	1 Kg.	140/-
31.	Divya Medohar Vati	50 g.	75/-
		100 g.	150/-
32.	Divya Shwasari Ras	20 g.	30/-
		50 g.	75/-
33.	Divya Shwasari Pravahi	500 g.	50/-
34.	Divya Stri Rasayan	20 g.	40/-
		60 g.	120/-

35.	Divya Hridyamrit	10 g.	50/-
		20 g.	100/-
		40 g.	200/-
36.	Divya Madhu-kalp Vati	40 g.	40/-
37.	Divya Vatari Choorna	50 g.	15/-
38.	Divya Shilajit Rasayan	20 g.	30/-
		40 g.	60/-
39.	Divya Sarvakalp Kvath	100 g.	20/-
40.	Divya Bel Sharbat	750 ml.	55/-
41.	Divya Badam Sharbat	750 ml.	90/-
42.	Divya Gulab Sharbat	750 ml.	65/-

BHASMAS (CALCINED POWDERS)

43.	Divya Abhrak Bhasm	10 g.	25/-
44.	Divya Akeek Pisthi	10 g.	30/-
45.	Divya Kapardak Bhasm	20 g.	20/-
46.	Divya Kaharawa Pishti	10 g.	80/-
47.	Divya Kasees Bhasm	20 g.	15/-
48.	Divya Godanti Bhasm	20 g.	10/-
49.	Divya Jahar-mohara Pishti	10 g.	30/-
50.	Divya Tankan Bhasm	10 g.	10/-
51.	Divya Tamra Bhasm	1 g.	7/-
52.	Divya Trivanga Bhasm	10 g.	50/-
53.	Divya Praval (root) Pishti	10 g.	30/-
54.	Divya Praval (branch) Pisthi	10 g.	80/-
55.	Divya B(V)ang Bhasm	10 g.	50/-
56.	Divya Mandoor Bhasm	10 g.	20/-
57.	Divya Mukta Pishti (1)	1 g.	50/-
58.	Divya Mukta Pishti (2)	1 g.	30/-
59.	Divya Ropya (Silver) Bhasm	1 g.	40/-
60.	Divya Swarna Bhasm	1 g.	1600/-
61.	Divya Shring Bhasm	10 g.	30/-
62.	Divya Lauh Bhasm	10 g.	25/-

63.	Divya Shankh Bhasm	10 g.	10/-
64.	Divya Swarna-makshik Bhasm	10 g.	25/-
65.	Divya Sphatik Bhasm	10 g.	15/-
66.	Divya Hajrool-yahood Bhasm	10 g.	30/-
67.	Divya Heerak (Diamond) Bhasm	10 g.	2000/-
68.	Divya Sangeyashad Pishti	10 g.	30/-
69.	Divya Mukta-shukti Bhasm	10 g.	25/-

RAS & RASAYAN (METALLIC PREPARATIONS & REJUVENATORS)

70.	Divya Kumar Kalyan Ras	1 g.	325/-
71.	Divya Yogendra Ras	1 g.	275/-
72.	Divya Vasantakusumakar	1 g.	200/-
73.	Divya Brihad Vata-chintamani	1 g.	250/-
74.	Divya Makardhwaj	1 g.	35/-
75.	Divya Swarna B(V)asantamalati	1 g.	125/-
76.	Divya Rasaraj Ras	1 g.	275/-
77.	Divya Amavatari Ras	20 g.	35/-
		40 g.	70/-
78.	Divya Ekangaveer Ras	10 g.	50/-
79.	Divya Kamadudha Ras (with pearls)	10 g.	25/-
80.	Divya Praval Panchamrit	5 g.	80/-
81.	Divya Mahavata Vidhvans Ras	10 g.	40/-
82.	Divya Ras Manikya	1 g.	5/-
		5 g.	25/-
83.	Divya Ras Sindoor	1 g.	7/-
84.	Divya Laxmi Vilas Ras	1 g.	30/-
		5 g.	60/-
85.	Divya Tribhuvan Kirti Ras	10 g.	25/-
		20 g.	50/-

VATI (TABLETS & PILLS)

86.	Divya Arogyawardhini Vati	10 g.	20/-
		20 g.	40/-

87.	Divya Kutaj-ghan vati	10 g.	15/-
		20 g.	30/-
88.	Divya Khadiradi Vati	10 g.	15/-
		20 g.	30/-
89.	Divya Chandraprabha Vati	20 g.	35/-
		60 g.	105/-
90.	Divya Chitrakadi Vati	10 g.	20/-
		20 g.	40/-
91.	Divya Rajahpravartani Vati	10 g.	25/-
		20 g.	50/-
92.	Divya Vishatinduk Vati	10 g.	20/-
		20 g.	40/-
93.	Divya Sanjeevani Vati	10 g.	20/-
		20 g.	40/-
94.	Divya Lavangadi Vati	10 g.	20/-
		20 g.	40/-
95.	Divya Vriddhivaadhika Vati	10 g.	20/-
		20 g.	40/-
96.	Divya Sarivadi Vati	10 g.	30/-
		20 g.	60/-

GUGGULU (Tablets Containing *Guggulu* or *Commiphara mukul* in Abundance)

97.	Divya Kanchanar Guggulu	20 g.	25/-
		60 g.	75/-
98.	Divya Kaishor Guggulu	20 g.	25/-
		60 g.	75/-
99.	Divya Gokshuradi Guggulu	20 g.	25/-
		60 g.	75/-
100.	Divya MahaYograj Guggulu	20 g.	45/-
		60 g.	135/-
101.	Divya Sinhanad Guggulu	20 g.	25/-
		60 g.	75/-

102.	Divya Yograj Guggulu	20 g.	25/-
		60 g.	75/-
103.	Divya Triphala Guggulu	20 g.	25/-
		60 g.	75/-
104.	Divya Saptavimshati Guggulu	20 g.	25/-
		60 g.	75/-
105.	Divya Lakshadi Guggulu	20 g.	25/-
106.	Divya Trayodashang Guggulu	20 g.	25/-
		60 g.	75/-

CHOORNA (Powder)

107.	Divya Ajamodadi Choorna	50 g.	15/-
		100 g.	30/-
108.	Divya Arjuna Choorna	100 g.	10/-
109.	Divya Avipattikar Choorna	50 g.	15/-
		100 g.	30/-
110.	Divya Ashwagandha Choorna	50 g.	15/-
		100 g.	30/-
111.	Divya Amala Choorna	100 g.	15/-
112.	Divya Panchakol Choorna	50 g.	20/-
113	Divya Mulethi Choorna	100 g.	15/-
114.	Divya Lavana-bhaskar Choorna	50 g.	15/-
		100 g.	30/-
115.	Divya Trikuta Choorna	50 g.	25/-
116.	Divya Swadisht Choorna	50 g.	15/-
		100 g.	30/-
117.	Divya Sitopaladi Choorna	25 g.	20/-
		100 g.	40/-
118.	Divya Triphala Choorna	100 g.	15/-
119.	Divya Gangadhar Choorna	50 g.	15/-

MISCELLANEOUS

120.	Divya Chyavan Prash (Linctus)	1 kg.	130/-
121.	Divya Chyavan Prash (with Saffron)	1 kg.	170/-
122.	Divya Amalaki Rasayan	50 g.	30/-
123.	Divya Shwet Parpati	10 g.	15/-
124.	Divya Punarnavadi Mandoor	10 g.	15/-
		20 g.	30/-
125.	Divya Giloy Sat	10 g.	15/-
126.	Divya Saptamrit Lauh	10 g.	20/-
127.	Divya Shuddh Shilajit Sat	20 g.	60/-
		50 g.	150/-
128.	Divya Dashamool Kvath	100 g.	10/
129.	Divya Maha Triphala Ghrit	200 g.	180/-
130.	Divya Kanti Lape	50 g.	30/-
131.	Divya Badampak	500 g.	225/-
132.	Divya Khadirarist	450 ml.	45/-
133.	Divya Amritastav	10 g.	20/-
134.	Divya Bavchi Churan	50 g.	20/-
135.	Divya Mahamanjishtharistha	450 ml.	45/-
136.	Divya Shila Sindur	1 g.	25/-
137.	Divya Kutjarist	450 ml.	45/-
138.	Divya Talsindur	1 g.	25/-
139.	Divya Totla Kwath	300 g.	30/-
140.	Divya Ashmriharkwath	300 g.	60/-
141.	Divya Kulya Bhasm Mixture	20 g.	60/-
142.	Divya Sarshvtaristh	450 ml.	65/-
143.	Divya Shivlinge Seed	1 g.	30/-
144.	Divya Putrajevak Seed	200 g.	30/-
145.	Divya Falghrit	200 g.	171/-
146.	Divya Ashwagandharistha	450 ml.	60/-

Comparative Price of Different Forms of Medicines (Through Graphic Charts)

Comparitive price of 'Churna' available in the market

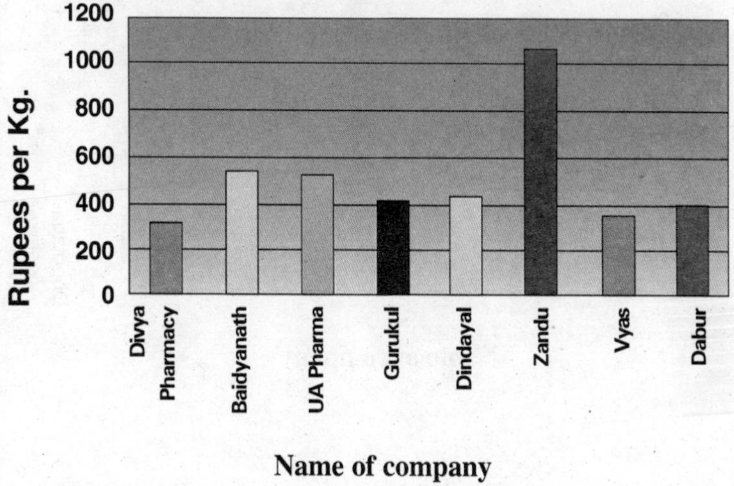

Comparitive price of 'Vati' available in the market

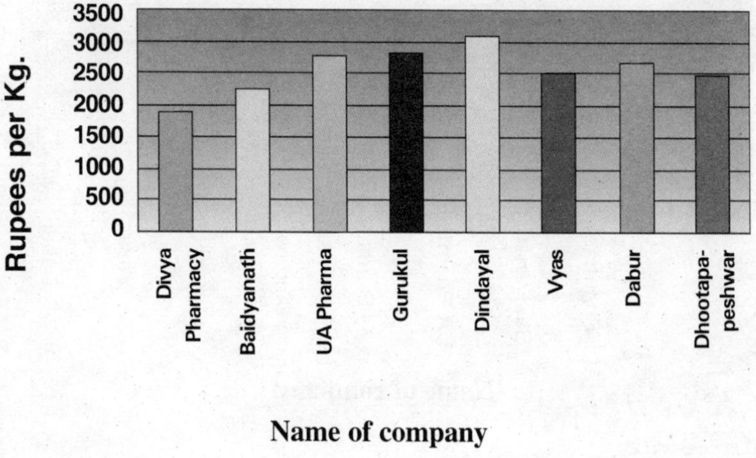

Comparitive price of 'Ras & Rasayan' available in the market

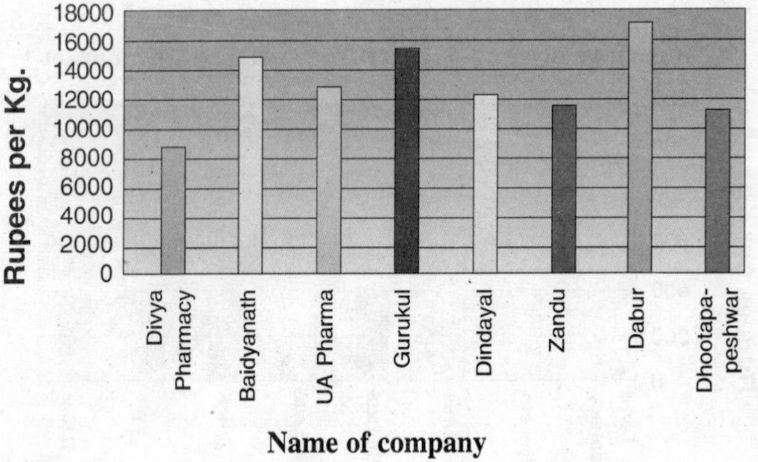

Comparitive price of 'Bhasm' available in the market

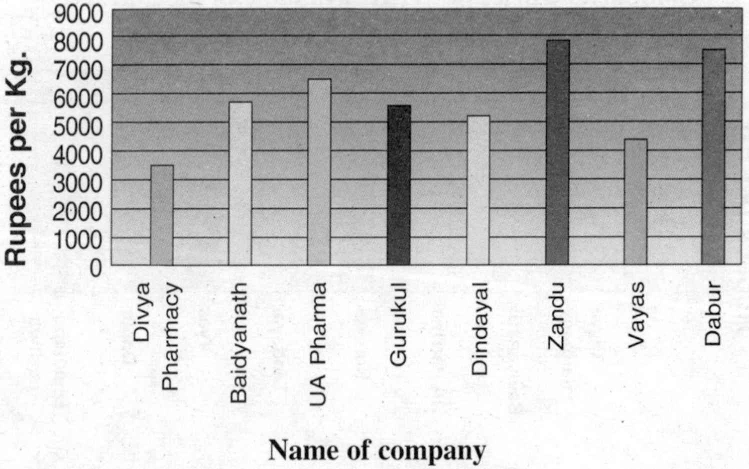

Comparitive price of 'Guggul' available in the market

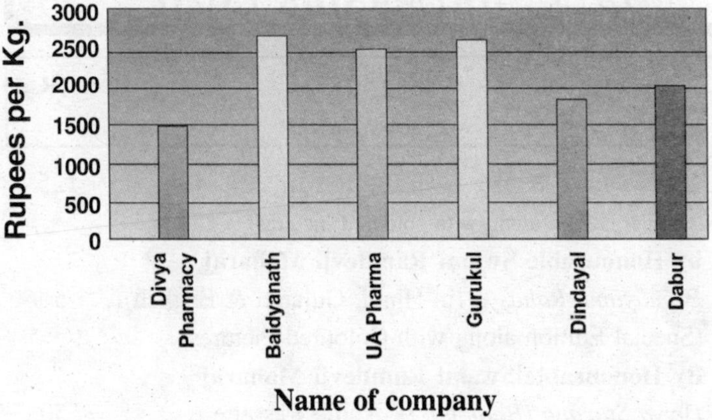

Comparitive price of 'Mukta Pisthi' 'Ropya, Swarna and Heerak Bhasmas available in the market

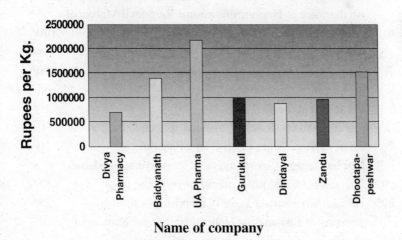

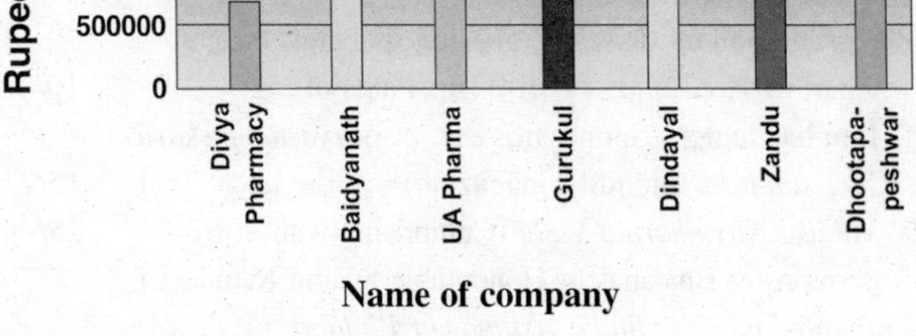

LIST OF YOGIC LITERATURE & AUDIO-VIDEO CASSETTES PUBLISHED BY *'DIVYA YOG MANDIR TRUST'*

S. No.	Name of Book	Rate (Rs.)
1.	*Yog Sādhanā & Yog Cikitsā Rahasya* (Special edition along with coloured pictures) **by Honourable Swami Ramdevji Maharaj**	125/-
2.	*Prāṇāyāma Rahasya* (in Hindi, Gujarati & English) (Special Edition along with Coloured Pictures) **By Honourable Swami Ramdevji Maharaj**	50/-
3.	*Divya Stavana (Bhajanas)* - Audio Cassette (Both First & Second Volumes) **(Bhajanas sung by Honourable Swami Ramdevji in the *Yog* Camps)**	50/-
4.	*Yog Nidrā* (Audio Cassatte)	30/-
5.	Chanting of *Gāyatrī Mantra & Mahā-mṛtuñjaya Mantra* (in the voice of **Honourable swami Ramdevji Maharaj**)	30/-
6.	*Divya Yog-Sādhanā (Āsanas & Prāṇāyāmas-* V.C.D.) 1-2 parts	150/-
7.	*Auṣadha-darśana* English (Revised edition)	50/-
	& All other languages	30/-
8.	Chart of *Yogāsanas* - Part-I (for abdominal diseases, obesity, diabetes, etc.)	10/-
9.	Chart of *Yogāsanas* - Part-2 (for Pains of Lumbar region, Spondylitis etc. & *Sūrya namaskāra*)	10/-
10.	*Yog-sandeśa* (monthly magazine)	15/-
11.	*Vaidika Nitya-karma Vidhi* (Comprising with Sermons & Bhajanas of Honourable Swami Ramdevji)	25/-
12.	*Jīvanī-śakti Vardhaka Aṣṭavarga Pādapa*	
13.	*Divya Auṣadhīya Sugandhita & Saundarya-karana paudha*	